RUNNING PRESS

GEM

MEASUREMENTS & CONVERSIONS

A Complete Guide

The Diagram Group

D0828882

Running Press
Philadelphia • London

First published in the United States of America in 1994 by
Running Press Book Publishers.

Copyright © 1993, 1994 by Diagram Visual Information Ltd

Originally published by HarperCollins Publishers Limited unde
title *Collins Gem Ready Reference*

20 19 18 17 16 15 14 13 12 11
Digit on the right indicates the number of this printing.

ISBN: 1-56138-466-6

Library of Congress Cataloging-in-Publication Number: 94-651

Cover design by Toby Schmidt

Printed in Great Britain by Omnia Books Ltd, Glasgow G64

This book may be ordered by mail from your publisher. Please
include $2.50 for postage and handling. *But try your bookstore f*

Running Press Book Publishers
125 South Twenty-second Street
Philadelphia, Pennsylvania 19103-4399

Foreword

Measurements are used to help establish the size of something. How far is it to the Moon? What is the page size of this book? How strong is the wind? So that these questions may be answered, many standards of measurement have been developed, encompassing things as diverse as radio wavelengths, wind speeds, earthquakes, and laundry codes. Different standards have been created around the world, and units based on both the US units/UK imperial and metric systems of measurement are now encountered. As a result, knowledge is needed of how to convert values from one system to another. The simple need to measure has created a complex web of units that now affects every aspect of life.

Measurements & Conversions is a uniquely useful guide to this world of measures. The book is divided into twelve sections, each providing essential information on the main units of measurement or features of a particular topic. When relevant, individual sections have conversion formulas, e.g. for metric and US units/UK imperial conversion equivalents, with conversion tables to provide immediate visual reference.

Measurements & Conversions is an indispensable, handy-sized guide to the international variety in units of measurement. It is an essential companion, whether for school, office, or home.

Contents

CONTENTS

5

How to use this book

Measurements & Conversions is divided into 12 sections, each of which is devoted to a particular category of facts and figures. If you know which category you wish to explore, merely turn to the table of contents to find the relevant page number.

Unit conversion index

In this book, there are tables for converting units from the US units/UK imperial system of measurement to the metric system (and vice versa), and for converting one type of unit to another within the same system. The Unit Conversion Index enables you to refer quickly to the tables in which a particular unit is converted.

Formulas

Within each section, you will find a selection of conversion formulas. These are easy-to-use formulas for common conversions; you will need to use a calculator for most of them, although many are simple, approximate conversions.

Conversion tables

Each group of units has its conversion tables: pages of quick-reference tables for all US units/UK imperial and metric measurements from meters to feet, grains to grams. These are particularly handy if you do not have a calculator. It would be impossible to accommodate tables listing every possible conversion, so the material included is not exhaustive.

You can use the following to convert figures larger than those in the table:

(**a**) separate the total into its parts: e.g., to convert 1,536

units of something, first convert the largest part in the table (1,000) and then each remaining part (500, 30, and 6). Then add these separate conversions together to find the total conversion; or
(b) move the decimal point in your original figure until it is at the same decimal place as those in the table. Look for the nearest number to this in the table and record the appropriate conversion. Then move the decimal point the same number of places in the opposite direction to give an approximate conversion of your original number.

Note also that the figures in the conversion tables are rounded up or down to the third decimal place, and so are not always exact.

Unit conversion index

Glossary

acre A measure of land: originally the amount of land that a yoke of oxen could plough in a day. Equal to 4,840 yd².

amu *see* Atomic mass unit.

ampere (A) The unit for measuring electric current.

ångström (Å) A unit of length, used mainly to measure the wavelength of light. Named for the Swedish physicist A.J. Ångström (1814–74). Equal to 10^{-10} m (10^{-8} cm).

apothecaries' system A system of weights used especially by pharmacists.

are (a) A unit of measure equal to an area of 10×10 m (1 a = 100 m²). *See also* Hectare (ha): 100 a = 1 ha.

astronomical unit (au or AU) A unit of measure based on the distance between the Earth and the Sun. Approximately equal to 1.5×10^8 km.

atomic mass unit (amu)

  chemical A unit of mass equal to $1/16$ of the weighted mass of the three naturally occurring neutral oxygen isotopes.
  1 amu chemical = $(1.660 \pm 0.00005) \times 10^{-27}$ kg.
  Formerly called the atomic weight unit.

  international A unit of mass equal to $1/12$ of the mass of a neutral carbon-12 atom. 1 amu international = $(1.66033 \pm 0.00005) \times 10^{-27}$ kg.

  physical A unit of mass equal to $1/16$ of the mass of an oxygen atom. 1 amu physical = 1.660×10^{-27} kg.

atto- In the US, a prefix meaning a quintillionth (10^{-18}); in the UK, meaning a trillionth (10^{-18}). For example, in the US, 1 attometer = 1 quintillionth of a meter, in the UK 1 attometer = 1 trillionth of a meter.

avoirdupois system A system of weights based on the 16-ounce pound and the 16-dram ounce.

baker's dozen A counting unit equal to 13.

barleycorn A unit of measure of length equal to $\frac{1}{3}$ in.

billion (bil) In the US, equal to 10^9; in UK, equal to 10^{12}. Commonly now also used in the UK to mean 10^9.

bolt A measure of length, usually for fabric. In the US, a bolt of wallpaper equals 16 yd and a bolt of cloth equals 40 yd; in the UK, a bolt of cloth equals 42 yd.

British thermal unit (Btu) Measure of heat needed to raise the temperature of 1 lb of water by 1 °F. Equal to 252 calories.

bushel (bu) A measure of dry volume. In the US, 1 bu = 8 gal (64 US pt); in the UK, 1 bu = 8 gal (64 UK pt). The measures are not to be confused: 1.03 US bu = 1 UK bu.

caliber A unit of length used to measure the diameter of a tube or the bore of a firearm, in $\frac{1}{100}$ in or $\frac{1}{1000}$ in increments.

calorie (cal) A measure of heat energy representing the amount of heat needed to raise 1 g of water by 1 °C. Also called "small calorie": 1,000 cal = 1 kcal or Cal. *See also* Joule; Kilocalorie.

carat A unit of weight equal to 200 mg (3.1 grains). Also used as a measure of gold purity (per 24 parts gold alloy).

centi- Prefix meaning a 100 or $\frac{1}{100}$; e.g., a centiliter (cl) is a unit of volume equal to $\frac{1}{100}$ (0.01) liter.

centrad A measure of a plane angle, especially used to measure the angular deviation of light through a prism. 1 centrad = $\frac{1}{100}$ (0.01) radian.

century A measure of time equal to 100 years.

chain A measure of length equal to 22 yd. Also known as Gunter's chain.

> **engineer's chain** A measure of length equal to 100 ft.
>
> **nautical chain** A measure of length equal to 15 ft.
>
> **square chain** A measure of area equal to 484 yd^2.

chaldron A measure of volume. In the US, 1 chaldron = 36 US bu; in the UK, 1 chaldron = 36 UK bu (288 gal).

cord A unit of dry volume, especially used for timber. Equal to 128 ft^3.

cubic units (cu or ^{3}) These are arrived at by multiplying a number by itself twice. With a three dimensional object, the height, width, and length are multiplied togther to give its volume, which is measured in cubic units.

cubit A unit of length approximately equal to 18 in. Originally based on the distance from the tip of the middle finger to the elbow.

cup A measure of volume (either liquid or solid) used especially in cooking. In the US, 1 cup = ½ US pt (16 tbsp); in the UK, 1 cup = ½ UK pt (16 tbsp). The two should not be confused: 1⅕ US cups = 1 UK cup.

day

> **mean solar day** A measure of time representing the interval between consecutive passages of the Sun across the meridian, averaged over 1 year.

1 day = 24 hr (86,400 s).

sidereal day A measure of time approximately equal to 23 hr, 56 min, 4.09 s. A sidereal day represents the time needed for one complete rotation of the Earth on its axis.

deca- Prefix meaning ten; e.g., a decameter is a measure of length equal to 10 m.

decade A measure of time equal to 10 years.

deci- Prefix meaning $\frac{1}{10}$; e.g., a deciliter (dl) is a measure of liquid volume equal to $\frac{1}{10}$ (0.01) liter.

decibel (dB) A measure of relative sound intensity.

deka- *see* Deca-.

degree (°)

    geometrical A unit of measure of plane angle equal to $\frac{1}{360}$ of the circumference of a circle (1 circle = 360°).

    temperature A measure of temperature difference representing a single division on the temperature scale. The centigrade scale has 100 equal degrees; the Fahrenheit scale has 212 equal degrees.

digit One of ten Arabic symbols representing numbers 0 to 9. Also used in astronomy as a unit of measure equal to $\frac{1}{12}$ the diameter of the Sun or Moon. Used in ancient Egypt as a measure of length: 1 digit = 1 finger width.

douzieme A unit of length equal to $\frac{1}{12}$ line.

dozen A counting unit equal to 12.

drachm A unit of mass in the apothecaries' system. 1 drachm = $\frac{1}{8}$ apothecaries' ounce (60 grains).

dram (dr) A unit of mass equal to $\frac{1}{16}$ oz.

    fluid dram A unit of liquid volume. In the US, 1 fl dr = $\frac{1}{8}$ US fl oz; in the UK, 1 fl dr = $\frac{1}{8}$ UK fl oz. The two should not be confused: 0.960759 US fl dr = 1 UK fl dr.

dry Used in US to distinguish measures of dry (solid) volume as opposed to liquid (fluid) volume. For example, in the US, 1 fl pt = ⅛ US gal; 1 dry pt = 1/64 US bu. 1 US dry pt ≈ 0.969 UK pt ≈ 1.163 US fl pt. In the UK, the pint measures both dry and liquid volume.

dyne A unit of force equal to that needed to produce acceleration of 1 cm per second in a mass of 1 g. Replaced by the newton (N): 1 dyne = 10^{-5} N.

electronvolt (eV) A unit of energy measurement representing the energy acquired by an electron in passing through a potential difference of 1 volt. 1 eV = $(1.6 \pm 0.00007) \times 10^{-19}$ J.

erg A unit of energy measurement equal to the energy produced by a force of 1 dyne through a distance of 1 cm. Replaced by the joule, 1 erg = 10^{-7} J.

exa- In the US, a prefix meaning 1 quintillion (10^{18}); in the UK, meaning 1 trillion (10^{18}).

fathom (fm) Unit of length, especially used to measure marine depth. 1 fm = 6 ft. Originally based on the span of two outstretched arms.

feet per minute A unit of velocity representing the number of feet traveled in 1 min.

femto- In the US, a prefix meaning 1 quadrillionth (10^{-15}); in the UK, meaning 1 thousand billionth (10^{-15}).

firkin A unit of volume, used especially to measure beer or ale. In the US, 1 firkin = 9.8 US gal; in the UK, 1 firkin = 9 UK gal.

fluid Used to distinguish units of liquid (fluid) volume as opposed to dry (solid) volume.

fluid dram *see* Dram.

fluid ounce *see* Ounce.

foot (ft) A unit of length equal to 12 in.

furlong (fur) Unit of length equal to ⅛ mi (660 ft).

gallon (gal) A unit of liquid volume. In the US, 1 gal = 8 US pt; in the UK, 1 gal = 8 UK pt. The two should not be confused: 1.2 US gal = 1 UK gal.

    Winchester wine gallon (WWG) A unit of volume used for wine, honey, or other liquids. Equal to 0.83 UK gal.

gauge A unit of length used to measure the diameter of a shotgun bore; e.g., 6-gauge equals 23.34 mm. Originally based on the number of balls, of certain size, contained in 1 lb of shot.

giga- In the US, a prefix meaning 1 billion (10^9); in the UK, meaning 1 thousand million (10^9). For example, in the US, 1 gigameter = 1 billion meters; in the UK, 1 gigameter = 1 thousand million meters.

gill A unit of liquid volume. In the US (gi), 1 gi = ¼ US fl pt; in UK, 1 gill = ¼ UK pt. The two should not be confused: ½ US gi = 1 UK gill.

grade (^{g}) A measure of plane angle in geometry. $1^{\mathrm{g}} = 0.9°$.

grain (gr) A unit of mass measurement, used especially in the apothecaries' system. 1 grain = ¹⁄₇,₀₀₀ lb (avoirdupois); 480 grains = 1 ounce troy; 24 grains = 1 pennyweight.

gram (g) A unit of mass or volume measurement. 1 g = 0.001 kg.

gross A counting measure equal to 144 (or 12 dozen).

hand A unit of length, used especially to measure horses' height. 1 hand = 4 in.

hectare (ha) A measure of area, usually of land, equal to 10,000 m².

hecto- Prefix meaning 100; e.g., a hectometer (hm) is a unit of length equal to 100 m.

hertz (Hz) A unit of frequency measurement equal to 1 cycle per second.

horsepower (hp) A unit of work representing the power needed to raise 550 lb by 1 ft in 1 s.

    metric horsepower A unit of power representing that needed to raise a 75-kg mass 1 m in 1 s.

hour (hr) A unit of time measurement equal to 60 min (3,600 s).

hundredweight (cwt) A unit of mass.

    1 hundredweight = 4 quarters; 1 hundredweight troy = 100 pounds troy

    long (UK) hundredweight (cwt) 1 hundredweight =112 lb.

    short (US) hundredweight (sh cwt) 1 short hundredweight = 100 lb.

inch (in) A unit of length equal to ½ ft.

inches per second A unit of velocity representing the number of inches traveled in 1 s.

joule (J) A unit of energy equal to the work done when a force of 1 newton is moved through a distance of 1 m. Used instead of calorie: 1 J = 0.239 cal. Named for J.P. Joule (1818–89).

keg A unit of volume, used especially for beer,

approximately equal to 30 gal. Also used as a measure of weight for nails, equal to 100 lb.

kelvin (K) A scale of temperature measurement in which each degree is equal to $\frac{1}{273.16}$ of the interval between 0 K (absolute zero) and the triple point of water. K = °C + 273.16. Named for William Thomson, Lord Kelvin (1824–1907).

kilo- Prefix meaning 1,000; e.g., a kilogram (kg) is a unit of volume measurement equal to 1,000 g.

kilocalorie (kcal or Cal) A unit of energy measurement representing the amount of heat required to raise 1 kg of water by 1 °C. Also called the "international calorie." 1 kcal = 1,000 cal. *See also* Calorie.

kilogram *see* Kilo-

kilometer (km) A unit of length equal to 1,000 m.

kiloparsec A unit of distance used to measure distance between galactic bodies. 1 kiloparsec = 3,260 light years (ly).

kilowatt (kW) A unit of power equal to 1,000 watts (W).

kilowatt-hour (kWh) A unit of energy equal to the energy expended when a power of 1 kW is used for 1 hr.

knot (kn) A nautical unit of speed measurement equal to the velocity at which 1 n mi is traveled in 1 hr. 1 kn = 6,076 ft per hour.

lakh An Indian counting unit equal to 100,000.

lambda (λ) A unit of volume measurement. 1 λ = 1 microliter (10^{-6} liter).

league A unit of length equal to 3 mi.

light year (ly) A unit of length (distance) representing the distance traveled by electromagnetic waves (light)

through space in 1 year. 1 light year = 9.4605×10^{12} km (or, in the US, 6 trillion miles; in the UK, 6 billion miles).

line A unit of length equal to ¹⁄₁₂ in; 4 lines = 1 barleycorn. It can also be used to measure button diameters, when 1 line = ¹⁄₄₀ in.

liter (l) A unit of volume measurement equal to the volume of 1 kg of water at its maximum density. 1 liter = 1,000 cm³.

magnum A measure of volume, used especially for wine or champagne. In the US, 1 magnum = ²⁄₅ US gal; in the UK, 1 magnum = ²⁄₅ UK gal.

mega- Prefix meaning 1 million; e.g., a megaton is a unit of weight equal to 1 million tons.

megahertz (MHz) A unit of frequency (for radio) equal to 1 million cycles per second.

meter (m) A unit of length equal to 100 cm.

meters per minute (m/min) A unit of velocity measurement representing the number of meters traveled in 1 min.

metric system A system of measurement based on the meter.

micro- Prefix meaning 1 millionth; e.g., a microliter is a unit of volume equal to 1 millionth of a liter.

micron (μm) A unit of length equal to ¹⁄₁,₀₀₀ (0.001) mm. Also called the micrometer.

mile (mi) A unit of length equal to 1,760 yd. Also called the statute mile in the UK.

> **nautical mile (n mi)** A unit of length used in navigation. In the UK, 1 n mi = 6,080 ft; in the metric system, 1 n mi (international) = 1,852 m.

Also called the geographical mile.

sea mile A unit of length distinguished from the nautical mile. 1 sea mile = 1,000 fathoms (6,000 ft).

miles per hour (mph) A unit of velocity representing the number of miles traveled in 1 hr.

millennium A period of time equal to 1,000 years.

milli- Prefix meaning 1 thousandth or $\frac{1}{1,000}$; e.g., 1 millimeter (mm) is a unit of length equal to $\frac{1}{1,000}$ (0.001) m.

minim A unit of volume, usually for liquids. In the US, 1 minim = $\frac{1}{480}$ US fl oz; in the UK, 1 minim = $\frac{1}{480}$ UK fl oz. The two should not be confused: 0.961 US minim = 1 UK minim.

minute

    geometric (') A unit of measure for plane angles. $1' = \frac{1}{60}°$.

    time (m or min) A unit of time measurement equal to 60 s. 60 min = 1 hr.

month

    lunar A unit of time equal to 4 weeks (2,419,200 s).

    sidereal *see* Year, sidereal.

    tropical *see* Year, tropical.

nano- In the US, a prefix meaning 1 billionth (10^{-9}); in the UK, meaning 1 thousand millionth (10^{-9}). For example, in the US, 1 nanometer = 1 billionth of a meter; in the UK, 1 nanometer = 1 thousand millionth of a meter.

nautical mile *see* Mile.

newton (N) A unit of force equal to that creating an acceleration of 1 m per second when applied to a mass of 1 kg. This unit has replaced the dyne:

$1 N = 10^5$ dynes. Named for Isaac Newton (1642–1727).

ohm (Ω) A unit of electrical resistance. One ohm equals the resistance across which a potential difference of 1 volt produces a current flow of 1 ampere. Named for G.S. Ohm (1787–1854).

ounce (oz) A unit of mass equal to $1/16$ lb.
    fluid ounce A unit of liquid volume measurement. In the US, 1 fl oz = $1/16$ US pt; in the UK, 1 fl oz = $1/20$ UK pt.
    metric ounce A unit of mass equal to 25 g. Also called a Mounce.
    ounce troy A unit of mass in the troy system. Equal to $1/12$ pound troy.

pace A unit of length/distance equal to 5 ft, used in ancient Rome.
palm A unit of length used in ancient Egypt, equal to the width of an average palm of the hand (4 digits).
parsec (pc) A unit of length used for measuring astronomical distances. 1 parsec = 3.26 light years (ly).
pascal (pa) A unit of pressure equal to the force of 1 N acting over an area of 1 m².
peck (pk) A unit of dry volume. In the US, 1 peck = 2 US gal; in the UK, 1 peck = 2 UK gal. The two should not be confused: 1.032 US peck ≈ 1 UK peck.
pennyweight (dwt) A unit of weight in the troy system equal to $1/20$ ounce troy (25 grains).
perch A unit of length equal to $5\frac{1}{2}$ yd. Also called a pole or a rod.
peta- In the US, a prefix meaning 1 quadrillion (10^{15});

in the UK, meaning 1 thousand billion (10^{15}).

pi (π) Symbol and name representing the ratio of a circle's circumference to its diameter. Its value is approximately 3.14.

pica A unit of length, used by printers, approximately equal to ⅙ in.

pico- In the US, a prefix meaning 1 trillionth (10^{-12}); in the UK, a prefix meaning 1 billionth (10^{-12}). For example, in the US, 1 picometre = 1 trillionth of a metre; in the UK, 1 picometre = 1 billionth of a metre.

pint (pt) A unit of volume. In the US, two kinds of pint are used: 1 fl pt = ⅛ US gal. In the UK, a pint measures either dry or liquid volume: 1 pt = ⅛ UK gal; ¹⁄₆₄ US bu = 1 dry pt. These two should not be confused: 1.2 US fl pt ≈ 1.03 US dry pt ≈ 1 UK pt.

point A unit of length, used especially by printers, approximately equal to ¹⁄₇₂ in.

pole Unit of length equal to 5½ yd. *See also* Perch; Rod.

pound (lb) A unit of mass equal to 453.59 g.

> **force pound** A unit of force equal to 32.174 poundals. Also called pound-force.
>
> **pound troy (lb tr)** A unit of mass in the troy system. 1 pound troy = 12 ounces troy.

poundal A unit of force equal to that needed to give an acceleration of 1 ft per second to a mass of 1 lb.

PSI Pounds per square inch: a unit for measuring pressure. 1 PSI equals the pressure resulting from a force of 1 force pound acting over an area of 1 in². *See also* Pound.

quart (qt) A unit of volume, usually for liquids. In the US, 1 qt = 2 US fl pt; in the UK, 1 qt = 2 UK pt. The two should not be confused: 1.2 US qt ≈ 1 UK qt.

dry quart (dry qt) A unit of measure for dry (solid) volume in US.

reputed quart A unit of volume, used especially for wine, equal to ⅙ of a Winchester wine gallon.

Winchester quart A unit of fluid volume equal to 2.5 liters.

quarter (qr)

mass quarter A unit of mass. In the US, 1 quarter = ¼ US ton (500 lb); in the UK, 1 quarter = ¼ UK hundredweight (28 lb).

quarter troy (qr tr) A unit of weight equal to 25 troy pounds.

volume quarter A unit of volume, in the US, equal to 8.24 US bu. In the UK, equal to 8 UK bu.

quintal (q) A unit of mass equal to 100 kg or 100 lb. Called the short hundredweight in the US.

rad A short form of radian, a unit of measure for plane angles. *See also* Centrad.

ream A unit of volume, used to measure paper in bulk. 1 ream equals about 500 sheets.

rod

area rod A unit of area equal to 30¼ yd². Also called a square perch or a square pole.

length rod A unit of length equal to 5½ yd. *See also* Perch; Pole.

rood A unit of area equal to ¼ acre (1210 yd²).

score A counting unit equal to 20.

scruple A unit of mass in apothecaries' system equal to 20 grains.

second A unit of time equal to ⅟₆₀ minute.

    geometric (') A measure of plane angle equal to ⅟₃₆₀° and ⅟₆₀".

    orbital A unit of time equal to ⅟₃₁,₅₅₇ of the tropical year 1900. Also called Ephemeris second.

    sidereal A unit of time equal to ⅟₈₆,₄₀₀ of the interval needed for one complete rotation of the Earth on its axis.

square units (sq or ²) These are arrived at by multiplying a number by itself once. To find the area of, e.g. a square or rectangle, length and width are multiplied together to give the area, which is measured in square units.

stere A unit of volume, especially used for measuring timber. 1 stere = 1 m³.

stone (st) A unit of mass used in the UK. 1 st = 14 lb.

tablespoon (tbsp) A unit of volume used in cooking and equal to 1.5 centiliters (3 tsp). 16 tbsp = 1 cup.

teaspoon (tsp) A unit of volume used in cooking and equal to 0.5 centiliter. 3 tsp = 1 tbsp.

tera- In the US, a prefix meaning 1 trillion (10¹²); in the UK, meaning 1 billion (10¹²). For example, in the US, 1 terameter = 1 trillion meters; in the UK, 1 terameter = 1 billion meters.

ton A unit of mass. In the US, 1 ton = 2,000 lb. Called a short ton in the UK. In the UK, 1 ton = 2,240 lb. Called a long ton in the US.

    ton troy (ton tr) A unit of mass equal to 2,000 pounds troy.

tonne (t) A unit of mass equal to 1,000 kg. Also called a metric ton.

tonne of coal equivalent A measure of energy production/consumption based on the premise that 1 tonne of coal provides 8,000 kilowatt-hours (kWh) of energy.

trillion In US, equal to 10^{12}; in UK, equal to 10^{18}.

troy system A system of mass measurement based on the 20-ounce pound and the 20-pennyweight ounce.

volt (V) A unit of electromotive force and potential difference. Equal to the difference in potential between two points of a conducting wire carrying a constant current of 1 ampere (A), when the power released between the points is 1 watt (W). Named for Alessandro Volta (1745–1827).

watt (W) A unit of power equal to that available when 1 J of energy is expended in 1 s.
1 W = 1 volt-ampere; 746 W = 1 horsepower (hp). Named for James Watt (1736–1819).

X-unit (x or XU) A unit of length used especially for measuring wavelength. 1 x-unit ≈ 10^{-3} ångström (10^{-13} m).

yard (yd) A unit of length equal to 3 ft (36 in).

yards per minute (ypm) A unit of velocity representing the number of yards traveled in 1 min.

year A unit of time measurement determined by the revolution of the Earth around the Sun.

    anomalistic year Equals the time interval between two consecutive passages of the Earth through its perihelion (365 days, 6 hr, 13 min, 53 s).

sidereal year Equals the time in which it takes the Earth to revolve around the Sun from one fixed point (usually a star) back to the same point (365 days, 6 hr, 9 min, 9 s).

tropical year Equals the time interval between two consecutive passages of the Sun, in one direction, through the Earth's equatorial plane (or from vernal equinox to vernal equinox; 365 days, 5 hr, 48 min, 46 s).

Unit sytems

International System of Units

The International System of Units (or Système
International d'Unités – SI) is the current form of the
metric system that has been in use since 1960. In the US,
the SI system is increasingly used in education, science,
and in everyday life.

The table opposite shows the common conversions from
the metric to the US system of units.

Base units

There are seven base units in SI:

Unit	Symbol	Quantity
meter	m	length/distance
kilogram	kg	mass
ampere	A	electric current
kelvin	K	thermodynamic temperature
candela	cd	luminosity
second	s (or sec)	time
mole	mol	amount of substance

Prefixes to use with SI units

Prefixes are added to each of the base units to indicate
multiples and submultiples of ten:

Submultiple/ multiple	Prefix	Symbol
10^{-6}	micro-	r
10^{-3}	milli-	m
10^{-2}	centi-	c
10^{-1}	deci-	d
10	deca-	da
10^2	hecto-	h
10^3	kilo-	k
10^6	mega-	M

Derived units

In addition, the SI system uses derived units. For example, velocity is given in meters per second (m/s, ms^{-1}). Other derived units in SI are referred to by special names: the watt (W) is a unit of power; the joule (J) is a unit of energy; and the newton (N) is a unit of force.

Common conversions

	Metric	US
Length		
1 millimeter (mm)		0.039 in.
1 centimeter (cm)		0.394 in.
1 meter (m)		3.281 ft = 1.094 yd
1 kilometer (km)		1094 yd = 0.621 mi
Area		
1 square millimeter (mm^2)		0.015 in.^{2}
1 square centimeter (cm^2)		0.155 in.^{2}
1 square meter (m^2)		10.764 ft^2 = 1.196 yd^2
1 hectare (ha)		2.471 acres = 0.00386 mi^2
1 square kilometer (km^2)		0.386 mi^2
Volume		
1 cubic centimeter (cm^3)		0.061 in.^{3}
1 cubic meter (m^3)		35.315 ft^3 = 1.308 yd^3 = 227.020 dry gal = 264 fl gal
1 milliliter (ml)		0.034 fl oz
1 centiliter (cl)		0.338 fl oz
1 liter (l)		2.113 fl pt = 1.056 fl qt = 0.264 fl gal
Weight		
1 gram (g)		0.035 oz
1 kilogram (kg)		2.205 lb = 35.28 oz
1 tonne (t)		1.102 tons = 2204.623 lb

1: Numbers

Named numbers

Many numbers have names. Some of these names are in everyday use, others apply in more specialized areas such as music and multiple births and for sums of money. Some names for specialized numbers have the same first part (prefix). These prefixes indicate the number to which the name refers.

Everyday use

$1/10$	Tithe
2	Pair, couple, brace
6	Half a dozen
12	Dozen
13	Baker's dozen
20	Score
50	Half century
100	Century
144	Gross

Musicians

1	Soloist
2	Duet
3	Trio
4	Quartet
5	Quintet
6	Sextet
7	Septet
8	Octet

Multiple births

2	Twins
3	Triplets
4	Quadruplets (quads)
5	Quintuplets (quints)
6	Sextuplets

Slang for money

1¢	Penny
5¢	Nickel
10¢	Dime
25¢	Quarter, two bits
$1	Buck

Numerical prefixes

Prefixes in numerical order

$1/10$	Deci-	**7**	Hept-, hepta-, sept-, septi-, septem-
$1/2$	Semi-, hemi-, demi-	**8**	Oct-, octa-, octo-
1	Uni-	**9**	Non-, nona-, ennea-
2	Bi-, di-	**10**	Dec-, deca-, deka-
3	Tri-, ter-	**11**	Hendeca-, undec-, undeca-
4	Tetra-, tetr-, tessera-, quadri-, quadr-	**12**	Dodeca-
5	Pent-, penta-, quinqu-, quinque-, quint-	**15**	Quindeca-
6	Sex-, sexi-, hex-, hexa-	**20**	Icos-, icosa-, icosi-

Prefixes in alphabetical order

Bi-,	**2**	Pent-, penta-	**5**
Dec-, deca-, deka-	**10**	Quadr-, quadri-	**4**
Deci-	**1/10**	Quindeca-	**15**
Demi-	**1/2**	Quinqu-, quinque-	**5**
Di-	**2**	Quint-	**5**
Dodeca-	**12**	Semi-	**1/2**
Ennea-	**9**	Sept-, septem-, septi-	**7**
Hemi-	**1/2**	Sex-, sexi-	**6**
Hendeca-	**11**	Ter-	**3**
Hept-, Hepta-	**7**	Tessera-	**4**
Hex-, hexa-	**6**	Tetr-, tetra-	**4**
Icos-, icosa-, icosi-	**20**	Tri-	**3**
Non-, nona-	**9**	Undec-, undeca-	**11**
Oct-, octa-, octo-	**8**	Uni-	**1**

Prefixes and their values

Prefixes in order of value	Value
*Atto-	0.000000000000000001
*Femto-	0.000000000000001
*Pico-	0.000000000001
*Nano-	0.000000001
*Micro-	0.000001
*Milli-	0.001
*Centi-	0.01
*Deci-	0.1
Semi-, hemi-, demi-	0.5
Uni-	1
Bi-, di-	2
Tri-, ter-	3
Tetra-, tetr-, tessera-, quadri-, quadr-	4
Pent-, penta-, quinqu-, quinque-, quint-	5
Sex-, sexi-, hex-, hexa-	6
Hept-, hepta-, sept-, septi-, septem-	7

* approved for use with the SI system

Prefixes in order of value	Value
Oct-, octa-, octo-	8
Non-, nona-, ennea-	9
Dec-, deca-, deka-	10
Hendeca-, undec-, undeca-	11
Dodeca-	12
Quindeca-	15
Icos-, icosa-, icosi-	20
Hect-, hecto-	100
*Kilo-	1,000
Myria-	10,000
*Mega-	1,000,000
*Giga-	1,000,000,000
*Tera-	1,000,000,000,000
*Peta-	1,000,000,000,000,000
*Exa-	1,000,000,000,000,000,000

Historic number systems
Different civilizations have developed their own
systems for writing numbers. Here we show numerals
from eight such systems.

	Roman	Arabic	Chinese	Hindu
1	I	١	一	२
2	II	٢	二	३
3	III	٣	三	३
4	IV	٤	四	४
5	V	٥	五	५
6	VI	٦	六	६
7	VII	٧	七	७
8	VIII	٨	八	८
9	IX	٩	九	९
10	X	١٠	十	२०
50	L	٥٠	五十	५०
100	C	١٠٠	百	२००
500	D	٥٠٠	五百	५००
1000	M	١٠٠٠	千	२०००

Babylonian	Egyptian	Hebrew	Japanese
𒁹	|	א	一
𒁹𒁹	||	ב	二
𒁹𒁹𒁹	|||	ג	三
𒁹𒁹𒁹𒁹	||||	ד	四
𒁹𒁹𒁹𒁹𒁹	||| ||	ה	五
𒁹𒁹𒁹 𒁹𒁹𒁹	||| |||	ו	六
𒁹𒁹𒁹𒁹 𒁹𒁹𒁹	|||| |||	ז	七
𒁹𒁹𒁹𒁹 𒁹𒁹𒁹𒁹	|||| ||||	ח	八
𒁹𒁹𒁹 𒁹𒁹𒁹 𒁹𒁹𒁹	||| ||| |||	ט	九
𒌋	∩	י	十
𒌋𒌋𒌋𒌋	∩∩∩	כ ל מ נ ס	五十
𒁹𒌋𒌋𒌋𒌋	𓏺	ק	百
𒁹𒁹𒁹 𒌋	𓏽𓏽𓏽	תק	五百
𒁹 𒌋	𓆼	אלף	千

Roman number system

The Roman numeral system is a method of notation in which the capitals are modeled on ancient Roman inscriptions. The numerals are represented by seven capital letters of the alphabet:

I	one
V	five
X	ten
L	fifty
C	one hundred
D	five hundred
M	one thousand

These letters are the foundation of the system; they are combined in order to form all numbers. If a letter is preceded by another of lesser value (e.g., IX), the value of the combined form is the difference between the values of each letter (e.g., IX = X (10) − I (1) = 9).

To determine the value of a string of Roman numbers (letters), find the pairs in the string (those beginning with a lower value) and determine their values, then add these to the values of the other letters in the string:

MCMXCI = M+CM+XC+I = 1,000+900+90+1 = 1991

A dash over a letter multiplies the value by 1,000 (e.g. $\overline{V}$ = 5,000).

1 I	12 XII	35 XXXV	100 C
2 II	13 XIII	40 XL	200 CC
3 III	14 XIV	45 XLV	300 CCC
4 IV or IIII	15 XV	50 L	400 CD
5 V	16 XVI	55 LV	500 D
6 VI	17 XVII	60 LX	600 DC
7 VII	18 XVIII	65 LXV	700 DCC
8 VIII	19 XIX	70 LXX	800 DCCC
9 IX	20 XX	75 LXXV	900 CM
10 X	25 XXV	80 LXXX	1000 M
11 XI	30 XXX	90 XC	2000 MM

Mathematical symbols

$+$	plus or positive	$\geqslant$	greater than or equal to
$-$	minus or negative	$\leqslant$	less than or equal to
$\pm$	plus or minus, positive or negative	$\gg$	much greater than
$\times$	multiplied by	$\ll$	much less than
$\div$	divided by	$\sqrt{}$	square root
$=$	equal to	∞	infinity
$\equiv$	identically equal to	$\propto$	proportional to
$\neq$	not equal to	Σ	sum of
$\not\equiv$	not identically equal to	Π	product of
$\approx$	approximately equal to	Δ	difference
$\sim$	of the order of or similar to	$\therefore$	therefore
$>$	greater than	$\angle$	angle
$<$	less than	$\parallel$	parallel to
$\not>$	not greater than	$\perp$	perpendicular to
$\not<$	not less than	$:$	is to

Arithmetic operations

The four basic arithmetic operations are addition, subtraction, multiplication, and division. Each part of an arithmetic operation has a specific name.

Addition

29 Addend
+6 Addend
35 Sum

Subtraction

74 Minuend
-16 Subtrahend
58 Difference

Multiplication

46 Multiplicand
x9 Multiplier
414 Product

Division

Divisor
Quotient 3
13)44 Dividend
39
5 Remainder

Fraction

5/8 5 Numerator
     8 Denominator

Simple (or vulgar) fraction

9/7 9 Numerator
     7 Denominator

Binary numbers

The binary system is formulated on a base of 2, or on a sum of powers of 2. For example, the number 101011 is equal to $2^5 + 0 + 2^3 + 0 + 2^1 + 2^0$; in the decimal system, this number equals 43. The system is used frequently in computer applications.

In describing computer storage, 1 bit = 1 binary digit; 1 byte = 8 bits in most systems; 1 megabyte (MB) = 1,048,576 bytes. The table below shows other decimal/binary equivalents.

Decimal	Binary	Decimal	Binary
1	1	21	10101
2	10	30	11110
3	11	40	101000
4	100	50	110010
5	101	60	111100
6	110	90	1011010
7	111	100	1100100
8	1000	200	11001000
9	1001	300	100101100
10	1010	400	110010000
11	1011	500	111110100
12	1100	600	1001011000
13	1101	900	1110000100
14	1110	1,000	1111101000
15	1111	2,000	11111010000
16	10000	4,000	111110100000
17	10001	5,000	1001110001000
18	10010	10,000	10011100010000
19	10011	20,000	100111000100000
20	10100	100,000	11000011010100000

Computer coding systems

ASCII (American Standard Code for Information Interchange) is an international coding system of character representation. Its 256 codes represent computer commands and letters of the alphabet. Hexadecimal is a system of numbering based on 16 digits (as opposed to 10 in the decimal system): 1 to 9 and A to F.

Binary, ASCII, and hexadecimal systems are used in computer programming.

The table below shows character equivalents in decimal, hexadecimal, and ASCII systems.

Dec	Hex	ASCII	Dec	Hex	ASCII
000	00	NUL	016	10	DLE
001	01	SOH	017	11	DC1
002	02	STX	018	12	DC2
003	03	ETX	019	13	DC3
004	04	EOT	020	14	DC4
005	05	ENQ	021	15	NAK
006	06	ACK	022	16	SYN
007	07	BEL	023	17	ETB
008	08	BS	024	18	CAN
009	09	HT	025	19	EM
010	0A	LF	026	1A	SUB
011	0B	VT	027	1B	ESCAPE
012	0C	FF	028	1C	FS
013	0D	CR	029	1D	GS
014	0E	SO	030	1E	RS
015	0F	SI	031	1F	US

Dec	Hex	ASCII	Dec	Hex	ASCII
032	20	SPACE	057	39	9
033	21	!	058	3A	:
034	22	"	059	3B	;
035	23	#	060	3C	<
036	24	$	061	3D	=
037	25	%	062	3E	>
038	26	&	063	3F	?
039	27	'	064	40	@
040	28	(	065	41	A
041	29	)	066	42	B
042	2A	*	067	43	C
043	2B	+	068	44	D
044	2C	,	069	45	E
045	2D	–	070	46	F
046	2E	.	071	47	G
047	2F	/	072	48	H
048	30	0	073	49	I
049	31	1	074	4A	J
050	32	2	075	4B	K
051	33	3	076	4C	L
052	34	4	077	4D	M
053	35	5	078	4E	N
054	36	6	079	4F	O
055	37	7	080	50	P
056	38	8	081	51	Q

Dec	Hex	ASCII
082	52	R
083	53	S
084	54	T
085	55	U
086	56	V
087	57	W
088	58	X
089	59	Y
090	5A	Z
091	5B	[
092	5C	\
093	5D	]
094	5E	^
095	5F	_
096	60	`
097	61	a
098	62	b
099	63	c
100	64	d
101	65	e
102	66	f
103	67	g
104	68	h
105	69	i
106	6A	j

Dec	Hex	ASCII
107	6B	k
108	6C	l
109	6D	m
110	6E	n
111	6F	o
112	70	p
113	71	q
114	72	r
115	73	s
116	74	t
117	75	u
118	76	v
119	77	w
120	78	x
121	79	y
122	7A	z
123	7B	{
124	7C		
125	7D	}
126	7E	~
127	7F	DEL

Fractions, decimals and percentages

Fraction			Decimal	Percentage
$1/9$			0.111111	11.11%
$1/7$			0.142857	14.29%
$1/6$			0.166667	16.67%
$1/5$			0.2	20.00%
$2/9$			0.222222	22.22%
$2/7$			0.285714	28.58%
$3/9$	$2/6$	$1/3$	0.333333	33.33%
$2/5$			0.4	40.00%
$3/7$			0.428571	42.86%
$4/9$			0.444444	44.44%
$3/6$			0.5	50.00%
$5/9$			0.555555	55.56%
$4/7$			0.571429	57.14%
$3/5$			0.6	60.00%
$6/9$	$4/6$	$2/3$	0.666666	66.67%
$5/7$			0.714286	71.43%
$7/9$			0.777778	77.78%
$4/5$			0.8	80.00%
$5/6$			0.833333	83.33%
$6/7$			0.857143	85.71%
$8/9$			0.888889	88.89%
$9/9$ $7/7$ $6/6$ $5/5$ $3/3$			1	100%

Fraction					Decimal	Percentage
$^1/_{64}$					0.015625	1.56%
$^2/_{64}$	$^1/_{32}$				0.03125	3.13%
$^3/_{64}$					0.046875	4.69%
$^4/_{64}$	$^2/_{32}$	$^1/_{16}$			0.0625	6.25%
$^5/_{64}$					0.078125	7.81%
$^6/_{64}$	$^3/_{32}$				0.09375	9.38%
$^7/_{64}$					0.109375	10.94%
$^8/_{64}$	$^4/_{32}$	$^2/_{16}$	$^1/_8$		0.125	12.50%
$^9/_{64}$					0.140625	14.06%
$^{10}/_{64}$	$^5/_{32}$				0.15625	15.63%
$^{11}/_{64}$					0.171875	17.19%
$^{12}/_{64}$	$^6/_{32}$	$^3/_{16}$			0.1875	18.75%
$^{13}/_{64}$					0.203125	20.31%
$^{14}/_{64}$	$^7/_{32}$				0.21875	21.88%
$^{15}/_{64}$					0.234375	23.44%
$^{16}/_{64}$	$^8/_{32}$	$^4/_{16}$	$^2/_8$	$^1/_4$	0.25	25.00%
$^{17}/_{64}$					0.265625	26.56%
$^{18}/_{64}$	$^9/_{32}$				0.28125	28.13%
$^{19}/_{64}$					0.296875	29.69%
$^{20}/_{64}$	$^{10}/_{32}$	$^5/_{16}$			0.3125	31.25%
$^{21}/_{64}$					0.328125	32.81%
$^{22}/_{64}$	$^{11}/_{32}$				0.34375	34.38%

Fractions, decimals and percentages (continued)

Fraction	Decimal	Percentage
$\frac{23}{64}$	0.359375	35.94%
$\frac{24}{64}$ $\frac{12}{32}$ $\frac{6}{16}$ $\frac{3}{8}$	0.375	37.50%
$\frac{25}{64}$	0.390625	39.06%
$\frac{26}{64}$ $\frac{12}{32}$	0.40625	40.63%
$\frac{27}{64}$	0.421875	42.19%
$\frac{28}{64}$ $\frac{14}{32}$ $\frac{7}{16}$	0.4375	43.75%
$\frac{29}{64}$	0.453125	45.31%
$\frac{30}{64}$ $\frac{15}{32}$	0.46875	46.88%
$\frac{31}{64}$	0.484375	48.44%
$\frac{32}{64}$ $\frac{16}{32}$ $\frac{8}{16}$ $\frac{4}{8}$ $\frac{2}{4}$ $\frac{1}{2}$	0.5	50.00%
$\frac{33}{64}$	0.515625	51.56%
$\frac{34}{64}$ $\frac{17}{32}$	0.53125	53.13%
$\frac{35}{64}$	0.546875	54.69%
$\frac{36}{64}$ $\frac{18}{32}$ $\frac{9}{16}$	0.5625	56.25%
$\frac{37}{64}$	0.578125	57.81%
$\frac{38}{64}$ $\frac{19}{32}$	0.59375	59.37%
$\frac{39}{64}$	0.609375	60.94%
$\frac{40}{64}$ $\frac{20}{32}$ $\frac{10}{16}$ $\frac{5}{8}$	0.625	62.50%
$\frac{41}{64}$	0.640625	64.06%
$\frac{42}{64}$ $\frac{21}{32}$	0.65625	65.63%
$\frac{43}{64}$	0.671875	67.19%
$\frac{44}{64}$ $\frac{22}{32}$ $\frac{11}{16}$	0.6875	68.75%

Fraction	Decimal	Percentage
$\frac{45}{64}$	0.703125	70.31%
$\frac{46}{64}$ $\frac{23}{32}$	0.71875	71.88%
$\frac{47}{64}$	0.734375	73.44%
$\frac{48}{64}$ $\frac{24}{32}$ $\frac{12}{16}$ $\frac{6}{8}$ $\frac{3}{4}$	0.75	75.00%
$\frac{49}{64}$	0.765625	76.56%
$\frac{50}{64}$ $\frac{25}{32}$	0.78125	78.13%
$\frac{51}{64}$	0.796875	79.69%
$\frac{52}{64}$ $\frac{26}{32}$ $\frac{13}{16}$	0.8125	81.25%
$\frac{53}{64}$	0.828125	82.81%
$\frac{54}{64}$ $\frac{27}{32}$	0.84375	84.38%
$\frac{55}{64}$	0.859375	85.94%
$\frac{56}{64}$ $\frac{28}{32}$ $\frac{14}{16}$ $\frac{7}{8}$	0.875	87.50%
$\frac{57}{64}$	0.890625	89.06%
$\frac{58}{64}$ $\frac{29}{32}$	0.90625	90.63%
$\frac{59}{64}$	0.921875	92.19%
$\frac{60}{64}$ $\frac{30}{32}$ $\frac{15}{16}$	0.9375	93.75%
$\frac{61}{64}$	0.953125	95.31%
$\frac{62}{64}$ $\frac{31}{32}$	0.96875	96.88%
$\frac{63}{64}$	0.984375	98.44%
$\frac{64}{64}$ $\frac{32}{32}$ $\frac{16}{16}$ $\frac{8}{8}$ $\frac{4}{4}$ $\frac{2}{2}$	1	100%

Prime numbers

These are whole numbers that have only two factors –
the number itself and the number 1. The only even
prime number is 2: all other prime numbers are odd.

There are an infinite number of prime numbers. The
first 126 are given below. The number at the foot of the
table is the largest prime known in 1952. The largest
prime known in 1983 has 39,751 digits.

2	47	109	191	269	353	439	523	617
3	53	113	193	271	359	443	541	619
5	59	127	197	277	367	449	547	631
7	61	131	199	281	373	457	557	641
11	67	137	211	283	379	461	563	643
13	71	139	223	293	383	463	569	647
17	73	149	227	307	389	467	571	653
19	79	151	229	311	397	479	577	659
23	83	157	233	313	401	487	587	661
29	89	163	239	317	409	491	593	673
31	97	167	241	331	419	499	599	677
37	101	173	251	337	421	503	601	683
41	103	179	257	347	431	509	607	691
43	107	181	263	349	433	521	613	701

170141183460469231731687303715884105727

Fibonacci sequence

Each number in a Fibonacci sequence is the sum of the two numbers preceding it. The sequence can therefore be built up using simple addition. Below is an example of a Fibonacci sequence.

$0 + 1 = \mathbf{1}$	$987 + 610 = \mathbf{1{,}597}$
$1 + 1 = \mathbf{2}$	$1{,}597 + 987 = \mathbf{2{,}584}$
$2 + 1 = \mathbf{3}$	$2{,}584 + 1{,}597 = \mathbf{4{,}181}$
$3 + 2 = \mathbf{5}$	$4{,}181 + 2{,}584 = \mathbf{6{,}765}$
$5 + 3 = \mathbf{8}$	$6{,}765 + 4{,}181 = \mathbf{10{,}946}$
$8 + 5 = \mathbf{13}$	$10{,}946 + 6{,}765 = \mathbf{17{,}711}$
$13 + 8 = \mathbf{21}$	$17{,}711 + 10{,}946 = \mathbf{28{,}657}$
$21 + 13 = \mathbf{34}$	$28{,}657 + 17{,}711 = \mathbf{46{,}368}$
$34 + 21 = \mathbf{55}$	$46{,}368 + 28{,}657 = \mathbf{75{,}025}$
$55 + 34 = \mathbf{89}$	$75{,}025 + 46{,}368 = \mathbf{121{,}393}$
$89 + 55 = \mathbf{144}$	$121{,}393 + 75{,}025 = \mathbf{196{,}418}$
$144 + 89 = \mathbf{233}$	$196{,}418 + 121{,}393 = \mathbf{317{,}811}$
$233 + 144 = \mathbf{377}$	$317{,}811 + 196{,}418 = \mathbf{514{,}229}$
$377 + 233 = \mathbf{610}$	$514{,}229 + 317{,}811 = \mathbf{832{,}040}$
$610 + 377 = \mathbf{987}$	$832{,}040 + 514{,}229 = \mathbf{1{,}346{,}269}$

Square and cube roots

*Accurate to 3 decimal places – they have not been rounded up or down.

Square and cube* roots of 1 to 25				Square and cube* roots of 26 to 50		
	$\sqrt{}$	$\sqrt[3]{}$			$\sqrt{}$	$\sqrt[3]{}$
1	1.000	1.000		26	5.099	2.962
2	1.414	1.259		27	5.196	3.000
3	1.732	1.442		28	5.291	3.036
4	2.000	1.587		29	5.385	3.072
5	2.236	1.709		30	5.477	3.107
6	2.449	1.817		31	5.567	3.141
7	2.645	1.912		32	5.656	3.174
8	2.828	2.000		33	5.744	3.207
9	3.000	2.080		34	5.831	3.239
10	3.162	2.154		35	5.916	3.271
11	3.316	2.223		36	6.000	3.301
12	3.464	2.289		37	6.082	3.332
13	3.605	2.351		38	6.164	3.361
14	3.741	2.410		39	6.245	3.391
15	3.873	2.466		40	6.324	3.419
16	4.000	2.519		41	6.403	3.448
17	4.123	2.571		42	6.480	3.476
18	4.242	2.620		43	6.557	3.503
19	4.358	2.668		44	6.633	3.530
20	4.472	2.714		45	6.708	3.556
21	4.582	2.758		46	6.782	3.583
22	4.690	2.802		47	6.855	3.608
23	4.795	2.843		48	6.928	3.634
24	4.899	2.884		49	7.000	3.659
25	5.000	2.924		50	7.071	3.684

Square and cube* roots of 51 to 75

	√	∛
51	7.141	3.708
52	7.211	3.732
53	7.280	3.756
54	7.348	3.779
55	7.416	3.802
56	7.483	3.825
57	7.549	3.848
58	7.615	3.870
59	7.681	3.893
60	7.746	3.913
61	7.810	3.936
62	7.874	3.957
63	7.937	3.979
64	8.000	4.000
65	8.062	4.020
66	8.124	4.041
67	8.185	4.061
68	8.246	4.081
69	8.306	4.101
70	8.366	4.121
71	8.426	4.140
72	8.485	4.160
73	8.544	4.179
74	8.602	4.198
75	8.660	4.217

Square and cube* roots of 76 to 100

	√	∛
76	8.717	4.235
77	8.775	4.254
78	8.831	4.272
79	8.888	4.290
80	8.944	4.308
81	9.000	4.326
82	9.055	4.344
83	9.110	4.362
84	9.165	4.379
85	9.219	4.396
86	9.273	4.414
87	9.327	4.431
88	9.380	4.447
89	9.434	4.464
90	9.486	4.481
91	9.539	4.497
92	9.591	4.514
93	9.643	4.530
94	9.695	4.546
95	9.746	4.562
96	9.798	4.578
97	9.848	4.594
98	9.899	4.610
99	9.949	4.626
100	10.000	4.641

Multiplication tables

×2		×3		×4		×5		×6	
1	2	1	3	1	4	1	5	1	6
2	4	2	6	2	8	2	10	2	12
3	6	3	9	3	12	3	15	3	18
4	8	4	12	4	16	4	20	4	24
5	10	5	15	5	20	5	25	5	30
6	12	6	18	6	24	6	30	6	36
7	14	7	21	7	28	7	35	7	42
8	16	8	24	8	32	8	40	8	48
9	18	9	27	9	36	9	45	9	54
10	20	10	30	10	40	10	50	10	60
11	22	11	33	11	44	11	55	11	66
12	24	12	36	12	48	12	60	12	72
13	26	13	39	13	52	13	65	13	78
14	28	14	42	14	56	14	70	14	84
15	30	15	45	15	60	15	75	15	90
16	32	16	48	16	64	16	80	16	96
17	34	17	51	17	68	17	85	17	102
18	36	18	54	18	72	18	90	18	108
19	38	19	57	19	76	19	95	19	114
25	50	25	75	25	100	25	125	25	150
35	70	35	105	35	140	35	175	35	210
45	90	45	135	45	180	45	225	45	270
55	110	55	165	55	220	55	275	55	330
65	130	65	195	65	260	65	325	65	390
75	150	75	225	75	300	75	375	75	450
85	170	85	255	85	340	85	425	85	510
95	190	95	285	95	380	95	475	95	570

×7		×8		×9		×10		×11	
1	7	1	8	1	9	1	10	1	11
2	14	2	16	2	18	2	20	2	22
3	21	3	24	3	27	3	30	3	33
4	28	4	32	4	36	4	40	4	44
5	35	5	40	5	45	5	50	5	55
6	42	6	48	6	54	6	60	6	66
7	49	7	56	7	63	7	70	7	77
8	56	8	64	8	72	8	80	8	88
9	63	9	72	9	81	9	90	9	99
10	70	10	80	10	90	10	100	10	110
11	77	11	88	11	99	11	110	11	121
12	84	12	96	12	108	12	120	12	132
13	91	13	104	13	117	13	130	13	143
14	98	14	112	14	126	14	140	14	154
15	105	15	120	15	135	15	150	15	165
16	112	16	128	16	144	16	160	16	176
17	119	17	136	17	153	17	170	17	187
18	126	18	144	18	162	18	180	18	198
19	133	19	152	19	171	19	190	19	209
25	175	25	200	25	225	25	250	25	275
35	245	35	280	35	315	35	350	35	385
45	315	45	360	45	405	45	450	45	495
55	385	55	440	55	495	55	550	55	605
65	455	65	520	65	585	65	650	65	715
75	525	75	600	75	675	75	750	75	825
85	595	85	680	85	765	85	850	85	935
95	665	95	760	95	855	95	950	95	1,045

Multiplication tables (continued)

×12		×13		×14		×15		×16	
1	12	1	13	1	14	1	15	1	16
2	24	2	26	2	28	2	30	2	32
3	36	3	39	3	42	3	45	3	48
4	48	4	52	4	56	4	60	4	64
5	60	5	65	5	70	5	75	5	80
6	72	6	78	6	84	6	90	6	96
7	84	7	91	7	98	7	105	7	112
8	96	8	104	8	112	8	120	8	128
9	108	9	117	9	126	9	135	9	144
10	120	10	130	10	140	10	150	10	160
11	132	11	143	11	154	11	165	11	176
12	144	12	156	12	168	12	180	12	192
13	156	13	169	13	182	13	195	13	208
14	168	14	182	14	196	14	210	14	224
15	180	15	195	15	210	15	225	15	240
16	192	16	208	16	224	16	240	16	256
17	204	17	221	17	238	17	255	17	272
18	216	18	234	18	252	18	270	18	288
19	228	19	247	19	266	19	285	19	304
25	300	25	325	25	350	25	375	25	400
35	420	35	455	35	490	35	525	35	560
45	540	45	585	45	630	45	675	45	720
55	660	55	715	55	770	55	825	55	880
65	780	65	845	65	910	65	975	65	1,040
75	900	75	975	75	1,050	75	1,125	75	1,200
85	1,020	85	1,105	85	1,190	85	1,275	85	1,360
95	1,140	95	1,235	95	1,330	95	1,425	95	1,520

×17		×18		×19		×20		×21	
1	17	1	18	1	19	1	20	1	21
2	34	2	36	2	38	2	40	2	42
3	51	3	54	3	57	3	60	3	63
4	68	4	72	4	76	4	80	4	84
5	85	5	90	5	95	5	100	5	105
6	102	6	108	6	114	6	120	6	126
7	119	7	126	7	133	7	140	7	147
8	136	8	144	8	152	8	160	8	168
9	153	9	162	9	171	9	180	9	189
10	170	10	180	10	190	10	200	10	210
11	187	11	198	11	209	11	220	11	231
12	204	12	216	12	228	12	240	12	252
13	221	13	234	13	247	13	260	13	273
14	238	14	252	14	266	14	280	14	294
15	255	15	270	15	285	15	300	15	315
16	272	16	288	16	304	16	320	16	336
17	289	17	306	17	323	17	340	17	357
18	306	18	324	18	342	18	360	18	378
19	323	19	342	19	361	19	380	19	399
25	425	25	450	25	475	25	500	25	525
35	595	35	630	35	665	35	700	35	735
45	765	45	810	45	855	45	900	45	945
55	935	55	990	55	1,045	55	1,100	55	1,155
65	1,105	65	1,170	65	1,235	65	1,300	65	1,365
75	1,275	75	1,350	75	1,425	75	1,500	75	1,575
85	1,445	85	1,530	85	1,615	85	1,700	85	1,785
95	1,615	95	1,710	95	1,805	95	1,900	95	1,995

Multiplication grid

Below is a quick-reference grid giving products and
quotients. It can be used for either multiplication or
division.

	Column											
Row	**1**	**2**	**3**	**4**	**5**	**6**	**7**	**8**	**9**	**10**	**11**	**12**
1	1	2	3	4	5	6	7	8	9	10	11	12
2	2	4	6	8	10	12	14	16	18	20	22	24
3	3	6	9	12	15	18	21	24	27	30	33	36
4	4	8	12	16	20	24	28	32	36	40	44	48
5	5	10	15	20	25	30	35	40	45	50	55	60
6	6	12	18	24	30	36	42	48	54	60	66	72
7	7	14	21	28	35	42	49	56	63	70	77	84
8	8	16	24	32	40	48	56	64	72	80	88	96
9	9	18	27	36	45	54	63	72	81	90	99	108
10	10	20	30	40	50	60	70	80	90	100	110	120
11	11	22	33	44	55	66	77	88	99	110	121	132
12	12	24	36	48	60	72	84	96	108	120	132	144

Multiplication

To multiply 6 by 9, for example, scan down column six
until you reach row nine. The number in the square
where column six intersects row nine is the product, 54.

Division

To divide 56 by 8, scan down column eight to find 56
(the dividend) then scan across to find the row number.
This is the quotient, 7.

Interest

Interest refers to the charge made for borrowing money or to payment given for investing money. It is usually expressed in terms of percentage rates. There are two types of interest: simple interest and compound interest.

Simple interest

This type of interest is calculated on the amount of money originally loaned (the principal). The formula used to calculate simple interest is:

$$I = \frac{P \times R \times T}{100}$$

I is interest, P is principal, R is the percentage rate per unit time, and T is the length of time (measured in units) over which the money is invested or loaned.

The final sum – or amount of money to which the principal will grow – is figured using the formula:

$$S \text{ (sum)} = P\left(1 + \frac{R \times T}{100}\right)$$

Compound interest

Unlike simple interest, which is paid only on the principal, compound interest is paid also on the previous interest earned. Thus the sum – or amount to which the principal will grow – increases at a much faster rate than with simple interest.

Compound interest is figured using the formula:

$$S = P(1 + i)^n$$

The "i" represents the periodic interest; "n" is the number of periods.

Simple interest

Simple interest rates (in dollars) to add to $1000 percent per annum				
Period	**2.5%**	**3%**	**3.5%**	**4%**
1 day	0.068	0.082	0.096	0.110
2 days	0.137	0.164	0.192	0.219
3 days	0.205	0.247	0.288	0.329
4 days	0.274	0.329	0.384	0.438
5 days	0.342	0.411	0.479	0.548
6 days	0.411	0.493	0.575	0.658
30 days	2.055	2.466	2.877	3.288
60 days	4.110	4.932	5.753	6.575
90 days	6.164	7.397	8.630	9.863
180 days	12.329	14.795	17.260	19.726
360 days	24.658	29.589	34.521	39.452
1 year	25.000	30.000	35.000	40.000

Simple interest (in dollars) added on to a principal of $100 percent per annum				
Period	**7%**	**8%**	**9%**	**10%**
1 year	107.00	108.00	109.00	110.00
5 years	135.00	140.00	145.00	150.00
10 years	170.00	180.00	190.00	200.00
20 years	240.00	260.00	280.00	300.00
30 years	310.00	340.00	370.00	400.00
40 years	380.00	420.00	460.00	500.00
50 years	450.00	500.00	550.00	600.00

percent per annum					
4.5%	**5%**	**5.5%**	**6%**	**6.5%**	**7%**
0.123	0.137	0.151	0.164	0.178	0.192
0.247	0.274	0.301	0.389	0.356	0.384
0.370	0.411	0.452	0.493	0.534	0.575
0.493	0.548	0.603	0.658	0.712	0.767
0.616	0.685	0.753	0.822	0.890	0.959
0.740	0.822	0.904	0.986	1.068	1.151
3.699	4.110	4.521	4.932	5.342	5.753
7.397	8.219	9.041	9.863	10.685	11.507
11.096	12.329	13.562	14.795	16.027	17.260
22.192	24.658	27.123	29.589	32.055	34.521
44.384	49.315	54.247	59.178	64.110	69.041
45.000	50.000	55.000	60.000	65.000	70.000

percent per annum				
11%	**12%**	**13%**	**14%**	**15%**
111.00	112.00	113.00	114.00	115.00
155.00	160.00	165.00	170.00	175.00
210.00	220.00	230.00	240.00	250.00
320.00	340.00	360.00	380.00	400.00
430.00	460.00	490.00	520.00	550.00
540.00	580.00	620.00	660.00	700.00
650.00	700.00	750.00	800.00	850.00

Compound interest

The table below shows the compound interest paid (in dollars) on a principal of $100. The interest rate is in percent per annum.

Period	4%	5%	6%	7%
1 day	0.011	0.014	0.016	0.019
1 week	0.077	0.096	0.115	0.135
6 months	2.00	2.50	3.00	3.50
1 year	4.00	5.00	6.00	7.00
2 years	8.16	10.25	12.36	14.49
3 years	12.49	15.76	19.10	22.50
4 years	16.99	21.55	26.25	31.08
5 years	21.67	27.63	33.82	40.26
6 years	26.53	34.01	41.85	50.07
7 years	31.59	40.71	50.36	60.58
8 years	36.86	47.75	59.38	71.82
9 years	42.33	55.13	68.95	83.85
10 years	48.02	62.89	79.08	96.72

Comparing the two

Money grows much more quickly with compound interest than with simple interest. Compare, for example, the amount of time required for an amount of money to double itself with simple interest and with compound interest:

8%	9%	10%	12%	14%	16%
0.022	0.025	0.027	0.033	0.038	0.044
0.154	0.173	0.192	0.231	0.269	0.308
4.00	4.50	5.00	6.00	7.00	8.00
8.00	9.00	10.00	12.00	14.00	16.00
16.64	18.81	21.00	25.44	29.96	34.56
25.97	29.50	33.10	40.49	48.15	56.09
36.05	41.16	46.41	57.35	68.90	81.06
46.93	53.86	61.05	76.23	92.54	110.03
58.69	67.71	77.16	97.38	119.50	143.64
71.38	82.80	94.87	121.07	150.23	182.62
85.09	99.26	114.36	147.60	185.26	227.84
99.90	117.19	135.79	177.31	225.19	280.30
115.89	136.74	159.37	210.58	270.72	341.14

Rate	Simple	Compound
7%	14 yrs, 104 days	10 yrs, 89 days
10%	10 yrs	7 yrs, 100 days

2: Length and area

Formulas: length

Below are listed the multiplication/division factors for
converting units of length from US units/UK imperial
units to metric, and vice versa. Note that two kinds of
factors are given: quick, for an approximate conversion
that can be made without a calculator; and accurate, for
an exact conversion.

Milli-inches (mils) Micrometers (µm)		**Quick**	**Accurate**
mils ⟶ µm		× 25	× 25.4
µm ⟶ mils		÷ 25	× 0.0394

Inches (in) Millimeters (mm)			
in ⟶ mm		× 25	× 25.4
mm ⟶ in		÷ 25	× 0.0394

Inches (in) Centimeters (cm)			
in ⟶ cm		× 2.5	× 2.54
cm ⟶ in		÷ 2.5	× 0.394

Feet (ft) Meters (m)			
ft ⟶ m		÷ 3.3	× 0.305
m ⟶ ft		× 3.3	× 3.281

Yards (yd) Meters (m)			
yd ⟶ m		÷ 1	× 0.914
m ⟶ yd		× 1	× 1.094

			Quick	**Accurate**

Fathoms (fm) Meters (m)

			Quick	**Accurate**
	fm → m		× 2	× 1.83
	m → fm		÷ 2	× 0.547

Chains (ch) Meters (m)

	Quick	**Accurate**
ch → m	× 20	× 20.108
m → ch	÷ 20	× 0.0497

Furlongs (fur) Meters (m)

	Quick	**Accurate**
fur → m	× 200	× 201.17
m → fur	÷ 200	× 0.005

Yards (yd) Kilometers (km)

	Quick	**Accurate**
yd → km	÷ 1000	× 0.00091
km → yd	× 1000	× 1093.6

Miles (mi) Kilometers (km)

	Quick	**Accurate**
mi → km	× 1.5	× 1.609
km → mi	÷ 1.5	× 0.621

Nautical miles (n mi) Miles (mi)

	Quick	**Accurate**
n mi → mi	× 1.2	× 1.151
mi → n mi	÷ 1.2	× 0.869

Nautical miles (n mi) Kilometers (km)

	Quick	**Accurate**
n mi → km	× 2	× 1.852
km → n mi	÷ 2	× 0.54

Conversion tables: length

The tables below can be used to convert units of length
from one measuring system to another. The first group
of tables converts US units/UK imperial units to

Milli-inches to Micrometers		Inches to Millimeters		Inches to Centimeters	
mils	μm	in	mm	in	cm
1	25.4	1	25.4	1	2.54
2	50.8	2	50.8	2	5.08
3	76.2	3	76.2	3	7.62
4	101.6	4	101.6	4	10.16
5	127.0	5	127.0	5	12.70
6	152.4	6	152.4	6	15.24
7	177.8	7	177.8	7	17.78
8	203.2	8	203.2	8	20.32
9	228.6	9	228.6	9	22.86
10	254.0	10	254.0	10	25.40
20	508.0	20	508.0	20	50.80
30	762.0	30	762.0	30	76.20
40	1,016.0	40	1,016.0	40	101.60
50	1,270.0	50	1,270.0	50	127.00
60	1,524.0	60	1,524.0	60	152.40
70	1,778.0	70	1,778.0	70	177.80
80	2,032.0	80	2,032.0	80	203.20
90	2,286.0	90	2,286.0	90	228.60
100	2,540.0	100	2,540.0	100	254.00

metric; the second, beginning on page 66, converts
metric to US units/UK imperial.

Feet to Meters		Yards to Meters		Fathoms to Meters	
ft	m	yd	m	fm	m
1	0.305	1	0.914	1	1.83
2	0.610	2	1.829	2	3.66
3	0.914	3	2.743	3	5.49
4	1.219	4	3.658	4	7.32
5	1.524	5	4.572	5	9.14
6	1.829	6	5.486	6	10.97
7	2.134	7	6.401	7	12.80
8	2.438	8	7.315	8	14.63
9	2.743	9	8.230	9	16.46
10	3.048	10	9.144	10	18.29
20	6.096	20	18.288	20	36.58
30	9.144	30	27.432	30	54.87
40	12.192	40	36.576	40	73.16
50	15.240	50	45.720	50	91.45
60	18.288	60	54.864	60	109.74
70	21.336	70	64.008	70	128.03
80	24.384	80	73.152	80	146.32
90	27.432	90	82.296	90	164.61
100	30.480	100	91.440	100	182.90

US units/UK imperial and metric units of length (continued)

Chains to Meters		Furlongs to Meters		Yards to Kilometers	
ch	**m**	**fur**	**m**	**yd**	**km**
1	20.108	1	201.17	100	0.091
2	40.216	2	402.34	200	0.183
3	60.324	3	603.50	300	0.274
4	80.432	4	804.67	400	0.366
5	100.540	5	1,005.84	500	0.457
6	120.648	6	1,207.01	600	0.549
7	140.756	7	1,408.18	700	0.640
8	160.864	8	1,609.34	800	0.731
9	180.972	9	1,810.51	900	0.823
10	201.080	10	2,011.68	1,000	0.914
20	402.160	20	4,023.36	2,000	1.829
30	603.240	30	6,035.04	3,000	2.743
40	804.320	40	8,046.72	4,000	3.658
50	1,005.400	50	10,058.40	5,000	4.572
60	1,206.480	60	12,070.08	6,000	5.486
70	1,407.560	70	14,081.76	7,000	6.401
80	1,608.640	80	16,093.44	8,000	7.315
90	1,809.720	90	18,105.12	9,000	8.230
100	2,010.800	100	20,116.80	10,000	9.144

Miles to Kilometers		Nautical miles to Miles		Nautical miles to Kilometers	
mi	km	n mi	mi	n mi	km
1	1.609	1	1.151	1	1.852
2	3.219	2	2.302	2	3.704
3	4.828	3	3.452	3	5.556
4	6.437	4	4.603	4	7.408
5	8.047	5	5.754	5	9.260
6	9.656	6	6.905	6	11.112
7	11.265	7	8.055	7	12.964
8	12.875	8	9.206	8	14.816
9	14.484	9	10.357	9	16.668
10	16.093	10	11.508	10	18.520
20	32.187	20	23.016	20	37.040
30	48.280	30	34.523	30	55.560
40	64.374	40	46.031	40	74.080
50	80.467	50	57.539	50	92.600
60	96.561	60	69.047	60	111.120
70	112.654	70	80.554	70	129.640
80	128.748	80	92.062	80	148.160
90	144.841	90	103.570	90	166.680
100	160.934	100	115.078	100	185.200

US units/UK imperial and metric units of length (continued)

Micrometers to Milli-inches		Millimeters to Inches		Centimeters to Inches	
μm	mils	mm	in	cm	in
1	0.039	1	0.039	1	0.394
2	0.079	2	0.079	2	0.787
3	0.118	3	0.118	3	1.181
4	0.157	4	0.157	4	1.575
5	0.197	5	0.197	5	1.969
6	0.236	6	0.236	6	2.362
7	0.276	7	0.276	7	2.756
8	0.315	8	0.315	8	3.150
9	0.354	9	0.354	9	3.543
10	0.394	10	0.394	10	3.937
20	0.787	20	0.787	20	7.874
30	1.181	30	1.181	30	11.811
40	1.575	40	1.575	40	15.748
50	1.969	50	1.969	50	19.685
60	2.362	60	2.362	60	23.622
70	2.756	70	2.756	70	27.559
80	3.150	80	3.150	80	31.496
90	3.543	90	3.543	90	35.433
100	3.937	100	3.937	100	39.370

Meters to Feet		**Meters to Yards**		**Meters to Fathoms**	
m	ft	m	yd	m	fm
1	3.281	1	1.094	1	0.547
2	6.562	2	2.187	2	1.093
3	9.843	3	3.281	3	1.640
4	13.123	4	4.374	4	2.187
5	16.404	5	5.468	5	2.734
6	19.685	6	6.562	6	3.280
7	22.966	7	7.655	7	3.827
8	26.247	8	8.749	8	4.374
9	29.528	9	9.843	9	4.921
10	32.808	10	10.936	10	5.467
20	65.617	20	21.872	20	10.935
30	98.425	30	32.808	30	16.402
40	131.234	40	43.745	40	21.870
50	164.042	50	54.681	50	27.337
60	196.850	60	65.617	60	32.805
70	229.659	70	76.553	70	38.272
80	262.467	80	87.489	80	43.740
90	295.276	90	98.425	90	49.207
100	328.084	100	109.361	100	54.674

US units/UK imperial and metric units of length (continued)

Meters to Chains		Meters to Furlongs		Kilometers to Yards	
m	ch	m	fur	km	yd
1	0.0497	1	0.005	1	1,093.6
2	0.0994	2	0.010	2	2,187.2
3	0.1491	3	0.015	3	3,280.8
4	0.1989	4	0.020	4	4,374.4
5	0.2487	5	0.025	5	5,468.0
6	0.2983	6	0.030	6	6,561.6
7	0.3481	7	0.035	7	7,655.2
8	0.3979	8	0.040	8	8,748.8
9	0.4476	9	0.045	9	9,842.4
10	0.4973	10	0.050	10	10,936.0
20	0.9946	20	0.099	20	21,872.0
30	1.4919	30	0.149	30	32,808.0
40	1.9893	40	0.199	40	43,744.0
50	2.4866	50	0.249	50	54,680.0
60	2.9839	60	0.298	60	65,616.0
70	3.4812	70	0.348	70	76,552.0
80	3.9785	80	0.398	80	87,488.0
90	4.4758	90	0.447	90	98,424.0
100	4.9731	100	0.497	100	109,360.0

Kilometers to Miles		Miles to Nautical miles		Kilometers to Nautical miles	
km	mi	mi	n mi	km	n mi
1	0.621	1	0.869	1	0.54
2	1.243	2	1.738	2	1.08
3	1.864	3	2.607	3	1.62
4	2.485	4	3.476	4	2.16
5	3.107	5	4.349	5	2.70
6	3.728	6	5.214	6	3.24
7	4.350	7	6.083	7	3.78
8	4.971	8	6.952	8	4.32
9	5.592	9	7.821	9	4.86
10	6.214	10	8.690	10	5.40
20	12.427	20	17.380	20	10.80
30	18.641	30	26.069	30	16.20
40	24.855	40	34.759	40	21.60
50	31.069	50	43.449	50	27.00
60	37.282	60	52.139	60	32.40
70	43.496	70	60.828	70	37.80
80	49.710	80	69.518	80	43.20
90	55.923	90	78.208	90	48.60
100	62.137	100	86.900	100	54.00

Formulas: area

Below are listed the multiplication/division factors for
converting units of area from US units/UK imperial
units to metric, and vice versa. Note that two kinds of
factors are given: quick, for an approximate conversion
that can be made without a calculator; and accurate, for
an exact conversion.

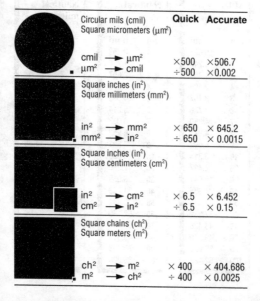

		Quick	**Accurate**
Circular mils (cmil) Square micrometers (μm^2)			
cmil $\longrightarrow$ μm^2		$\times 500$	$\times 506.7$
μm^2 $\longrightarrow$ cmil		$\div 500$	$\times 0.002$
Square inches (in^2) Square millimeters (mm^2)			
in^2 $\longrightarrow$ mm^2		$\times 650$	$\times 645.2$
mm^2 $\longrightarrow$ in^2		$\div 650$	$\times 0.0015$
Square inches (in^2) Square centimeters (cm^2)			
in^2 $\longrightarrow$ cm^2		$\times 6.5$	$\times 6.452$
cm^2 $\longrightarrow$ in^2		$\div 6.5$	$\times 0.15$
Square chains (ch^2) Square meters (m^2)			
ch^2 $\longrightarrow$ m^2		$\times 400$	$\times 404.686$
m^2 $\longrightarrow$ ch^2		$\div 400$	$\times 0.0025$

	Quick	Accurate
Square miles (mi²)		
Square kilometers (km²)		
mi² ⟶ km²	× 2.5	× 2.590
km² ⟶ mi²	÷ 2.5	× 0.386

Square miles (mi²)		
Hectares (ha)		
mi² ⟶ ha	× 250	× 258.999
ha ⟶ mi²	÷ 250	× 0.0039

Hectares (ha)		
Acres		
ha ⟶ acre	× 2.5	× 2.471
acre ⟶ ha	÷ 2.5	× 0.405

Square meters (m²)		
Square yards (yd²)		
m² ⟶ yd²	× 1	× 1.196
yd² ⟶ m²	÷ 1	× 0.836

Square meters (m²)		
Square feet (ft²)		
m² ⟶ ft²	× 11	× 10.764
ft² ⟶ m²	÷ 11	× 0.093

Conversion tables: area

The tables below can be used to convert units of area from one measuring system to another. The first group of tables converts US units/UK imperial units to

Circular mils to Square micrometers		Square inches to Square millimeters		Square inches to Square centimeters	
cmil	μm²	in²	mm²	in²	cm²
1	506.7	1	645.2	1	6.452
2	1,013.4	2	1,290.4	2	12.903
3	1,520.1	3	1,935.6	3	19.355
4	2,026.8	4	2,580.8	4	25.806
5	2,533.5	5	3,226.0	5	32.258
6	3,040.2	6	3,871.2	6	38.710
7	3,546.9	7	4,516.4	7	45.161
8	4,053.6	8	5,161.6	8	51.613
9	4,560.3	9	5,806.8	9	58.064
10	5,067.0	10	6,452.0	10	64.516
20	10,134.0	20	12,904.0	20	129.032
30	15,201.0	30	19,356.0	30	193.548
40	20,268.0	40	25,808.0	40	258.064
50	25,335.0	50	32,260.0	50	322.580
60	30,402.0	60	38,712.0	60	387.096
70	35,469.0	70	45,164.0	70	451.612
80	40,536.0	80	51,616.0	80	516.128
90	45,603.0	90	58,068.0	90	580.644
100	50,670.0	100	64,520.0	100	645.160

metric; the second, beginning on page 75, converts metric to US units/UK imperial.

Square feet to Square meters		Square yards to Square meters		Square chains to Square meters	
ft²	m²	yd²	m²	ch²	m²
1	0.093	1	0.836	1	404.686
2	0.186	2	1.672	2	809.372
3	0.279	3	2.508	3	1,214.058
4	0.372	4	3.345	4	1,618.744
5	0.465	5	4.181	5	2,023.430
6	0.557	6	5.017	6	2,428.116
7	0.650	7	5.853	7	2,832.802
8	0.743	8	6.689	8	3,237.488
9	0.836	9	7.525	9	3,642.174
10	0.929	10	8.361	10	4,046.860
20	1.858	20	16.723	20	8,093.720
30	2.787	30	25.084	30	12,140.580
40	3.716	40	33.445	40	16,187.440
50	4.645	50	41.806	50	20,234.300
60	5.574	60	50.168	60	24,281.160
70	6.503	70	58.529	70	28,328.020
80	7.432	80	66.890	80	32,374.880
90	8.361	90	75.251	90	36,421.740
100	9.290	100	83.613	100	40,468.600

US units/UK imperial and metric units of length (continued)

Acres to Hectares		Square miles to Hectares		Square miles to Square kilometers	
acre	ha	mi²	ha	mi²	km²
1	0.405	1	258.999	1	2.590
2	0.809	2	517.998	2	5.180
3	1.214	3	776.997	3	7.770
4	1.619	4	1,035.996	4	10.360
5	2.023	5	1,294.995	5	12.950
6	2.428	6	1,553.994	6	15.540
7	2.833	7	1,812.993	7	18.130
8	3.237	8	2,071.992	8	20.720
9	3.642	9	2,330.991	9	23.310
10	4.047	10	2,589.990	10	25.900
20	8.094	20	5,179.980	20	51.800
30	12.141	30	7,769.970	30	77.700
40	16.187	40	10,359.960	40	103.600
50	20.234	50	12,949.950	50	129.499
60	24.281	60	15,539.940	60	155.399
70	28.328	70	18,129.930	70	181.299
80	32.375	80	20,719.920	80	207.199
90	36.422	90	23,309.910	90	233.099
100	40.469	100	25,899.900	100	258.999

Square micrometers to Circular mils		Square millimeters to Square inches		Square centimeters to Square inches	
µm²	cmil	mm²	in²	cm²	in²
1	0.002	1	0.0015	1	0.155
2	0.004	2	0.0031	2	0.310
3	0.006	3	0.0047	3	0.465
4	0.008	4	0.0062	4	0.620
5	0.010	5	0.0078	5	0.775
6	0.012	6	0.0093	6	0.930
7	0.014	7	0.0109	7	1.085
8	0.016	8	0.0124	8	1.240
9	0.018	9	0.0140	9	1.395
10	0.020	10	0.0155	10	1.550
20	0.040	20	0.0310	20	3.100
30	0.060	30	0.0465	30	4.650
40	0.080	40	0.0620	40	6.200
50	0.100	50	0.0775	50	7.750
60	0.120	60	0.0930	60	9.300
70	0.140	70	0.1085	70	10.850
80	0.160	80	0.1240	80	12.400
90	0.180	90	0.1395	90	13.950
100	0.200	100	0.1550	100	15.500

US units/UK imperial and metric units of length (continued)

Square meters to Square feet		Square meters to Square yards		Square meters to Square chains	
m²	ft²	m²	yd²	m²	ch²
1	10.764	1	1.196	1	0.002
2	21.528	2	2.392	2	0.004
3	32.292	3	3.588	3	0.006
4	43.056	4	4.784	4	0.008
5	53.820	5	5.980	5	0.010
6	64.583	6	7.176	6	0.012
7	75.347	7	8.372	7	0.014
8	86.111	8	9.568	8	0.016
9	96.875	9	10.764	9	0.018
10	107.639	10	11.960	10	0.020
20	215.278	20	23.920	20	0.040
30	322.917	30	35.880	30	0.060
40	430.556	40	47.840	40	0.080
50	538.196	50	59.800	50	0.100
60	645.835	60	71.759	60	0.120
70	753.474	70	83.719	70	0.140
80	861.113	80	95.679	80	0.160
90	968.752	90	107.639	90	0.180
100	1,076.391	100	119.599	100	0.200

Hectares to Acres		Hectares to Square miles		Square kilometers to Square miles	
ha	acre	ha	mi²	km²	mi²
1	2.471	1	0.00386	1	0.386
2	4.942	2	0.00772	2	0.772
3	7.413	3	0.01158	3	1.158
4	9.884	4	0.01544	4	1.544
5	12.355	5	0.01931	5	1.931
6	14.826	6	0.02317	6	2.317
7	17.297	7	0.02703	7	2.703
8	19.768	8	0.03089	8	3.089
9	22.239	9	0.03475	9	3.475
10	24.711	10	0.03861	10	3.861
20	49.421	20	0.07722	20	7.722
30	74.132	30	0.11583	30	11.583
40	98.842	40	0.15444	40	15.444
50	123.553	50	0.19305	50	19.305
60	148.263	60	0.23166	60	23.166
70	172.974	70	0.27027	70	27.027
80	197.684	80	0.30888	80	30.888
90	222.395	90	0.34749	90	34.749
100	247.105	100	0.38610	100	38.610

Geometry of area

ABBREVIATIONS
a = length of top
b = length of base
h = perpendicular height
r = length of radius

$$\pi = 3.1416$$

Circle

$$\pi \times r^2$$

Rectangle

$$b \times h$$

Parallelogram

$$b \times h$$

Triangle

$$\frac{1}{2} \times b \times h$$

Trapezoid

$$\frac{(a + b)\, h}{2}$$

Geometry of surface area

ABBREVIATIONS
b = breadth of base
h = perpendicular height
l = length of base
r = length of radius

$$\pi = 3.1416$$

Cube

$$h \times b \times 6$$

Prism

$$(b \times h) + (3 \times l \times b)$$

Cylinder

$$(2 \times \pi \times r \times l) + (2 \times \pi \times r^2)$$

Pyramid

$$(2 \times b \times h) + (b^2)$$

Sphere

$$4 \times \pi \times r^2$$

3: Volume

Formulas

Below are listed the multiplication/division factors for converting units of volume from one measuring system to another. Note that two kinds of factors are given: quick, for an approximate conversion that can be made without a calculator; and accurate, for an exact conversion.

		Quick	Accurate
1 1	US fluid gallons (fl gal) UK gallons (gal)		
	US fl gal → UK gal	÷ 1	× 0.833
	UK gal → US fl gal	× 1	× 1.201
1 1	US fluid quarts (fl qt) UK quarts (qt)		
	US fl qt → UK qt	÷ 1	× 0.833
	UK qt → US fl qt	× 1	× 1.201
1 1	US fluid pints (fl pt) UK pints (pt)		
	US fl pt → UK pt	÷ 1	× 0.833
	UK pt → US fl pt	× 1	× 1.201
1 1	US fluid ounces (fl oz) UK fluid ounces (fl oz)		
	US fl oz → UK fl oz	÷ 1	× 1.041
	UK fl oz → US fl oz	× 1	× 0.961
1 16	Cubic inches (in³) Cubic centimetres (cm³)		
	in³ → cm³	× 16	× 16.387
	cm³ → in³	÷ 16	× 0.061

1 **35**	Cubic meters (m³) Cubic feet (ft³)			
	m³ ⟶ ft³	× 35	× 35.315	
	ft³ ⟶ m³	÷ 35	× 0.028	
1 **1**	Cubic meters (m³) Cubic yards (yd³)			
	m³ ⟶ yd³	× 1	× 1.308	
	yd³ ⟶ m³	÷ 1	× 0.765	
1 **30**	US fluid ounces (fl oz) Milliliters (ml)			
	US fl oz ⟶ ml	× 30	× 29.572	
	ml ⟶ US fl oz	÷ 30	× 0.034	
1 **4**	US fluid gallons (fl gal) Liters (l)			
	US fl gal ⟶ l	× 4	× 3.785	
	l ⟶ US fl gal	÷ 4	× 0.264	
1 **2**	Liters (l) US fluid pints (fl pt)			
	l ⟶ US fl pt	× 2	× 2.113	
	US fl pt ⟶ l	÷ 2	× 0.473	
1 **1**	Liters (l) US fluid quarts (fl qt)			
	l ⟶ US fl qt	× 1	× 1.056	
	US fl qt ⟶ l	÷ 1	× 0.947	
1 **264**	Cubic meters (m³) US fluid gallons (fl gal)			
	m³ ⟶ US fl gal	× 264	× 264.173	
	US fl gal ⟶ m³	÷ 264	× 0.004	

		Quick	**Accurate**
1 **227**	Cubic meters (m³) US dry gallons (dry gal)		
	m³ ⟶ dry gal	× 227	× 227.020
	dry gal ⟶ m³	÷ 227	× 0.004
1 **2**	UK fluid ounces (fl oz) Cubic inches (in³)		
	UK fl oz ⟶ in³	× 2	× 1.734
	in³ ⟶ UK fl oz	÷ 2	× 0.577
1 **28**	UK fluid ounces (fl oz) Milliliters (ml)		
	UK fl oz ⟶ ml	× 28	× 28.413
	ml ⟶ UK fl oz	÷ 28	× 0.035
1 **1**	UK quarts (qt) Liters (l)		
	UK qt ⟶ l	× 1	× 1.137
	l ⟶ UK qt	÷ 1	× 0.880
1 **4.5**	UK gallons (gal) Liters (l)		
	UK gal ⟶ l	× 4.5	× 4.546
	l ⟶ UK gal	÷ 4.5	× 0.220
1 **2**	Liters (l) UK pints (pt)		
	l ⟶ UK pt	× 2	× 1.760
	UK pt ⟶ l	÷ 2	× 0.568
1 **220**	Cubic meters (m³) UK gallons (gal)		
	m³ ⟶ UK gal	× 220	× 219.970
	UK gal ⟶ m³	÷ 220	× 0.005

Conversion tables
The tables below can be used to convert units of volume from one measuring system to another. The first group of tables, beginning below, converts US units to UK imperial units; the second, beginning on page 85, converts UK imperial units to US units.

US fluid gallons to UK gallons		US fluid quarts to UK quarts	
US fl gal	UK gal	US fl qt	UK qt
1	0.833	1	0.833
2	1.665	2	1.665
3	2.498	3	2.498
4	3.331	4	3.331
5	4.164	5	4.164
6	4.998	6	4.996
7	5.829	7	5.829
8	6.662	8	6.662
9	7.494	9	7.494
10	8.327	10	8.327
20	16.654	20	16.654
30	24.981	30	24.981
40	33.308	40	33.308
50	41.635	50	41.635
60	49.962	60	49.962
70	58.289	70	58.289
80	66.616	80	66.616
90	74.943	90	74.943
100	83.270	100	83.270

US units to UK imperial units conversions (continued)

US fluid pints to UK pints	
US fl pt	UK pt
1	0.833
2	1.665
3	2.498
4	3.331
5	4.164
6	4.996
7	5.829
8	6.662
9	7.494
10	8.327
20	16.654
30	24.981
40	33.308
50	41.635
60	49.962
70	58.289
80	66.616
90	74.943
100	83.270

US fluid ounces to UK fluid ounces	
US fl oz	UK fl oz
1	1.041
2	2.082
3	3.122
4	4.163
5	5.204
6	6.245
7	7.286
8	8.327
9	9.367
10	10.408
20	20.816
30	31.224
40	41.632
50	52.040
60	62.448
70	72.856
80	83.264
90	93.672
100	104.080

UK imperial units to US units conversions
The conversion tables below are used to convert UK
imperial units of volume to US units; tables beginning
on page 87 convert US units to metric units.

UK gallons to US fluid gallons		UK quarts to US fluid quarts	
UK gal	**US fl gal**	**UK qt**	**US fl qt**
1	1.201	1	1.201
2	2.402	2	2.402
3	3.603	3	3.603
4	4.804	4	4.804
5	6.005	5	6.005
6	7.206	6	7.206
7	8.407	7	8.407
8	9.608	8	9.608
9	10.809	9	10.809
10	12.010	10	12.010
20	24.020	20	24.020
30	36.030	30	36.030
40	48.040	40	48.040
50	60.050	50	60.050
60	72.060	60	72.060
70	84.070	70	84.070
80	96.080	80	96.080
90	108.090	90	108.090
100	120.100	100	120.100

UK imperial to US units conversions (continued)

UK pints to US fluid pints	
UK pt	**US fl pt**
1	1.201
2	2.402
3	3.603
4	4.804
5	6.005
6	7.206
7	8.407
8	9.608
9	10.809
10	12.010
20	24.020
30	36.030
40	48.040
50	60.050
60	72.060
70	84.070
80	96.080
90	108.090
100	120.100

UK fluid ounces to US fluid ounces	
UK fl oz	**US fl oz**
1	0.961
2	1.922
3	2.882
4	3.843
5	4.804
6	5.765
7	6.726
8	7.686
9	8.647
10	9.608
20	19.216
30	28.824
40	38.432
50	48.040
60	57.648
70	67.256
80	76.864
90	86.472
100	96.080

US units to metric conversions

The conversion tables below are used to convert US units of volume to metric units; tables beginning on page 95 convert metric units to US units.

US fluid ounces to Milliliters		US fluid pints to Liters		US fluid quarts to Liters	
US fl oz	ml	US fl pt	l	US fl qt	l
1	29.572	1	0.473	1	0.947
2	59.145	2	0.946	2	1.894
3	88.717	3	1.420	3	2.840
4	118.289	4	1.893	4	3.787
5	147.862	5	2.366	5	4.734
6	177.434	6	2.839	6	5.681
7	207.006	7	3.312	7	6.628
8	236.579	8	3.785	8	7.575
9	266.152	9	4.259	9	8.521
10	295.724	10	4.732	10	9.468
20	591.447	20	9.464	20	18.937
30	887.171	30	14.195	30	28.405
40	1,182.894	40	18.927	40	37.873
50	1,478.618	50	23.659	50	47.341
60	1,774.341	60	28.391	60	56.810
70	2,070.065	70	33.123	70	66.278
80	2,365.788	80	37.854	80	75.746
90	2,661.512	90	42.586	90	85.215
100	2,957.235	100	47.318	100	94.683

US units to metric conversions (continued)

US fluid gallons to Liters		US fluid gallons to Cubic meters		US dry gallons to Cubic meters	
US fl gal	l	US fl gal	m³	US dry gal	m³
1	3.785	1	0.004	1	0.004
2	7.571	2	0.008	2	0.009
3	11.356	3	0.011	3	0.013
4	15.141	4	0.015	4	0.018
5	18.927	5	0.019	5	0.022
6	22.712	6	0.023	6	0.026
7	26.497	7	0.026	7	0.031
8	30.282	8	0.030	8	0.035
9	34.068	9	0.034	9	0.040
10	37.853	10	0.038	10	0.044
20	75.706	20	0.076	20	0.088
30	113.559	30	0.114	30	0.132
40	151.412	40	0.151	40	0.176
50	189.265	50	0.189	50	0.220
60	227.118	60	0.227	60	0.264
70	264.971	70	0.265	70	0.308
80	302.824	80	0.303	80	0.352
90	340.677	90	0.341	90	0.396
100	378.530	100	0.379	100	0.440

Metric to US units conversions
The tables below convert metric units to US units.

Milliliters to US fluid ounces		Liters to US fluid pints		Liters to US fluid quarts	
ml	US fl oz	l	US fl pt	l	US fl qt
1	0.034	1	2.113	1	1.056
2	0.068	2	4.227	2	2.112
3	0.101	3	6.340	3	3.168
4	0.135	4	8.454	4	4.225
5	0.169	5	10.567	5	5.281
6	0.203	6	12.680	6	6.337
7	0.237	7	14.794	7	7.393
8	0.271	8	16.907	8	8.449
9	0.304	9	19.020	9	9.505
10	0.338	10	21.134	10	10.562
20	0.676	20	42.268	20	21.123
30	1.014	30	63.401	30	31.685
40	1.353	40	84.535	40	42.246
50	1.691	50	105.669	50	52.808
60	2.029	60	126.803	60	63.369
70	2.367	70	147.937	70	73.931
80	2.705	80	169.070	80	84.493
90	3.043	90	190.204	90	95.054
100	3.382	100	211.338	100	105.616

Metric to US units conversions (continued)

Liters to US fluid gallons		Cubic meters to US fluid gallons		Cubic meters to US dry gallons	
l	US fl gal	m³	US fl gal	m³	US dry gal
1	0.264	1	264.173	1	227.020
2	0.528	2	528.346	2	454.041
3	0.793	3	792.519	3	681.061
4	1.057	4	1,056.692	4	908.081
5	1.321	5	1,320.865	5	1,135.102
6	1.585	6	1,585.038	6	1,362.122
7	1.849	7	1,849.211	7	1,589.143
8	2.113	8	2,113.385	8	1,816.163
9	2.378	9	2,377.558	9	2,043.183
10	2.642	10	2,641.731	10	2,270.204
20	5.283	20	5,283.462	20	4,540.407
30	7.925	30	7,925.192	30	6,810.611
40	10.567	40	10,566.923	40	9,080.814
50	13.209	50	13,208.653	50	11,351.018
60	15.850	60	15,850.383	60	13,621.221
70	18.492	70	18,492.115	70	15,891.425
80	21.134	80	21,133.846	80	18,161.628
90	23.775	90	23,775.578	90	20,431.832
100	26.417	100	26,417.308	100	22,702.036

UK imperial to metric conversions
The conversion tables below are used to convert UK imperial units of volume to cubic units and metric units; tables beginning on page 94 convert metric units to UK imperial units.

UK fluid ounces to Cubic inches UK		Cubic inches to Cubic centimeters		Cubic feet to Cubic meters	
fl oz	in³	in³	cm³	ft³	m³
1	1.734	1	16.387	1	0.028
2	3.468	2	32.774	2	0.057
3	5.202	3	49.161	3	0.085
4	6.935	4	65.548	4	0.113
5	8.669	5	81.935	5	0.142
6	10.403	6	98.322	6	0.170
7	12.137	7	114.709	7	0.198
8	13.871	8	131.096	8	0.227
9	15.605	9	147.484	9	0.255
10	17.339	10	163.871	10	0.283
20	34.677	20	327.741	20	0.566
30	52.016	30	491.612	30	0.850
40	69.355	40	655.482	40	1.133
50	86.694	50	819.353	50	1.416
60	104.032	60	983.224	60	1.699
70	121.371	70	1,147.094	70	1.982
80	138.710	80	1,310.965	80	2.266
90	156.048	90	1,474.835	90	2.549
100	173.387	100	1,638.706	100	2.832

UK imperial to metric conversions (continued)

Cubic yards to Cubic meters		UK gallons to Cubic meters		UK gallons to Liters	
yd³	m³	UK gal	m³	UK gal	l
1	0.765	1	0.005	1	4.546
2	1.529	2	0.009	2	9.092
3	2.294	3	0.014	3	13.638
4	3.058	4	0.018	4	18.184
5	3.823	5	0.023	5	22.730
6	4.587	6	0.027	6	27.277
7	5.352	7	0.032	7	31.823
8	6.116	8	0.036	8	36.369
9	6.881	9	0.041	9	40.915
10	7.646	10	0.045	10	45.461
20	15.291	20	0.091	20	90.922
30	22.937	30	0.136	30	136.383
40	30.582	40	0.182	40	181.844
50	38.228	50	0.227	50	227.305
60	45.873	60	0.273	60	272.765
70	53.519	70	0.318	70	318.226
80	61.164	80	0.364	80	363.687
90	68.810	90	0.409	90	409.148
100	76.455	100	0.455	100	454.609

UK quarts to Liters	
UK qt	l
1	1.137
2	2.273
3	3.410
4	4.546
5	5.683
6	6.819
7	7.956
8	9.092
9	10.229
10	11.365
20	22.730
30	34.096
40	45.461
50	56.826
60	68.191
70	79.556
80	90.922
90	102.287
100	113.652

UK pints to Liters	
UK pt	l
1	0.568
2	1.137
3	1.705
4	2.273
5	2.841
6	3.410
7	3.978
8	4.546
9	5.114
10	5.683
20	11.365
30	17.048
40	22.730
50	28.413
60	34.096
70	39.778
80	45.461
90	51.143
100	56.826

UK fluid ounces to Milliliters	
UK fl oz	ml
1	28.413
2	56.826
3	85.239
4	113.652
5	142.065
6	170.478
7	198.891
8	227.305
9	255.718
10	284.131
20	568.261
30	852.392
40	1,136.523
50	1,420.654
60	1,704.784
70	1,988.915
80	2,273.046
90	2,557.177
100	2,841.307

Metric to UK imperial conversions
The tables below convert metric units to UK imperial units.

Milliliters to UK fluid ounces		Liters to UK pints		Liters to UK quarts	
ml	UK fl oz	l	UK pt	l	UK qt
1	0.035	1	1.760	1	0.880
2	0.070	2	3.520	2	1.760
3	0.106	3	5.279	3	2.640
4	0.141	4	7.039	4	3.520
5	0.176	5	8.799	5	4.399
6	0.211	6	10.559	6	5.279
7	0.246	7	12.318	7	6.159
8	0.282	8	14.078	8	7.039
9	0.317	9	15.838	9	7.919
10	0.352	10	17.598	10	8.799
20	0.704	20	35.195	20	17.598
30	1.056	30	52.793	30	26.396
40	1.408	40	70.390	40	35.195
50	1.760	50	87.988	50	43.994
60	2.112	60	105.585	60	52.793
70	2.464	70	123.183	70	61.591
80	2.816	80	140.780	80	70.390
90	3.168	90	158.378	90	79.189
100	3.520	100	175.975	100	87.988

Liters to UK gallons		Cubic meters to UK gallons		Cubic meters to Cubic feet	
l	UK gal	m³	UK gal	m³	ft³
1	0.220	1	219.970	1	35.315
2	0.440	2	439.940	2	70.629
3	0.660	3	659.909	3	105.944
4	0.880	4	879.879	4	141.259
5	1.100	5	1,099.849	5	176.573
6	1.320	6	1,319.818	6	211.888
7	1.540	7	1,539.788	7	247.203
8	1.760	8	1,759.757	8	282.517
9	1.980	9	1,979.727	9	317.832
10	2.200	10	2,199.697	10	353.147
20	4.399	20	4,399.396	20	706.293
30	6.599	30	6,599.093	30	1,059.440
40	8.799	40	8,798.789	40	1,412.587
50	10.999	50	10,998.485	50	1,765.734
60	13.198	60	13,198.181	60	2,118.880
70	15.398	70	15,397.877	70	2,472.027
80	17.598	80	17,597.573	80	2,825.174
90	19.797	90	19,797.269	90	3,178.320
100	21.997	100	21,996.965	100	3,531.467

Metric to UK imperial conversions (continued)

Cubic meters to Cubic yards		Cubic centimeters to Cubic inches		Cubic inches to UK fluid ounces	
m³	yd³	cm³	in³	in³	UK fl oz
1	1.308	1	0.061	1	0.577
2	2.616	2	0.122	2	1.153
3	3.924	3	0.183	3	1.730
4	5.232	4	0.244	4	2.307
5	6.540	5	0.305	5	2.884
6	7.848	6	0.366	6	3.460
7	9.156	7	0.427	7	4.037
8	10.464	8	0.488	8	4.614
9	11.772	9	0.549	9	5.191
10	13.080	10	0.610	10	5.767
20	26.159	20	1.220	20	11.535
30	39.239	30	1.831	30	17.302
40	52.318	40	2.441	40	23.069
50	65.398	50	3.051	50	28.837
60	78.477	60	3.661	60	34.604
70	91.557	70	4.271	70	40.371
80	104.636	80	4.882	80	46.138
90	117.716	90	5.492	90	51.906
100	130.795	100	6.102	100	57.673

Geometry of volume
ABBREVIATIONS
b = width of base
h = perpendicular height
l = length of base
r = length of radius

$$\pi = 3.1416$$

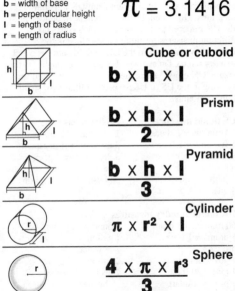

Cube or cuboid

$$b \times h \times l$$

Prism

$$\frac{b \times h \times l}{2}$$

Pyramid

$$\frac{b \times h \times l}{3}$$

Cylinder

$$\pi \times r^2 \times l$$

Sphere

$$\frac{4 \times \pi \times r^3}{3}$$

Cone

$$\frac{\pi \times r^2 \times h}{3}$$

Cooking measures

Although the names of the units are often the same, US measures are slightly different from UK imperial measures – for example, the US pint is 16 ounces, and the UK imperial pint is 20 ounces. US cooks use different measures for liquids and solids; in the imperial system used in the UK, a fluid ounce is equal to a dry ounce. On average, US units are roughly 4/5 the size of UK units. Metric measures are rarely used for cooking in the US or UK, except milliliters for small liquid amounts.

US liquid measures
60 minims = 1 fl dram
8 fl drams = 1 fl oz
4 fl oz = 1 gill
4 gills = 1 pint
2 pints = 1 quart
4 quarts = 1 gallon

US dry measures
1 dry pint = 1/2 dry quart
2 dry pints = 1 dry quart
8 dry quarts = 1 peck
4 pecks = 1 bushel
36 bushels = 1 chaldron

UK liquid and dry measures
60 minims = 1 dram
8 drams = 1 fl oz
5 fl oz = 1 gill
1 gill = 1/4 pint
1 pint = 20 fl oz
2 pints = 1 quart

4 quarts = 1 gallon
1 gallon = 10 lb (weight in water)
2 gallons = 1 peck
4 pecks = 1 bushel
36 bushels = 1 chaldron

Water weights
1 fl oz water = 1 oz
1 pint water = 1 lb

1 quart water = 2 lb
1 gallon water = 8 lb

Handy measures

Object	US units	Metric
1 thimbleful	30 drops	2.5 ml
60 drops	1 teaspoon	5 ml
1 teaspoon	1 fl dram	5 ml
1 dessertspoon	2 fl drams	10 ml
1 tablespoon	4 fl drams	15 ml
2 tablespoons	1 fl oz	30 ml
4 tablespoons	2 fl oz	60 ml
1 wine glass	4 fl oz (1 gill)	120 ml
1 cup	8 fl oz (½ pint)	240 ml

Beverage measures

Beer measures

1 nip = 1/4 pint	1 barrel = 31 1/2 gallons
1 small = 1/2 pint	1 hogshead = 2 barrels
1 large = 1 pint	1 butt = 2 hogsheads
1 flagon = 1 quart	1 tun = 2 butts
1 anker = 10 gallons	252 gallons
1 firkin = 9.8 gallons	

Handy measures
small jigger = 1 fl oz
small wine
  glass = 2 fl oz
sherry glass = 2 fl oz
cocktail glass = 1/4 pint
large wine
  glass = 1/4 pint
tumbler = 1/2 pint

Wine measures
10 gallons = 1 anker
1 hogshead = 63 gallons
2 hogsheads = 1 pipe
2 pipes = 1 tun
1 puncheon = 84 gallons
1 butt = 126 gallons

US spirits measures

1 shot = 1 fl oz	1 quart = 32 shots
1 pony = 1 shot	1 1/4 fifths
1 jigger = 1 1/2 shots	1 magnum
1 pint = 16 shots	of wine = 2 fifths
1 fifth = 25.6 shots	2 bottles
1.6 pints	
0.8 quart	
0.758 liter	

Champagne bottle sizes

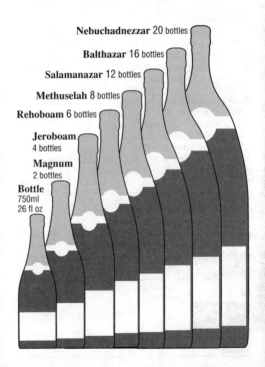

Nebuchadnezzar 20 bottles

Balthazar 16 bottles

Salamanazar 12 bottles

Methuselah 8 bottles

Rehoboam 6 bottles

Jeroboam
4 bottles

Magnum
2 bottles

Bottle
750ml
26 fl oz

4: Weight

Formulas

Below are listed the multiplication/division factors for converting units of weight from one measuring system to another. Note that two kinds of factors are given: quick, for an approximate conversion that can be made without a calculator; and accurate, for an exact conversion. The term "weight" differs in everyday use from its scientific use. In everyday terms, we use weight to describe how much substance an object has. In science, the term "mass" is used to describe this quantity of matter. Weight is used to describe the gravitational force on an object and is equal to its mass multiplied by the gravitational field strength. In scientific terms, mass remains constant but weight varies according to the strength of gravity. All units that follow are strictly units of mass rather than weight, apart from the pressure units kg/cm^2 and PSI.

			Quick	**Accurate**
	Grams (g) Grains (gr)			
	g ⟶ gr		× 15	× 15.432
	gr ⟶ g		÷ 15	× 0.065
	Ounces (oz) Grams (g)			
	oz ⟶ g		× 28	× 28.349
	g ⟶ oz		÷ 28	× 0.035

	Quick	Accurate
Ounces troy (oz tr)		
Grams (g)		
oz tr → g	× 31	× 31.103
g → oz tr	÷ 31	× 0.032
Stones (st)		
Kilograms (kg)		
st → kg	× 6	× 6.350
kg → st	÷ 6	× 0.157
Long (UK) tons (l t)		
Tonnes (t)		
l t → t	× 1	× 1.016
t → l t	÷ 1	× 0.984
Kilograms (kg)		
Pounds (lb)		
kg → lb	× 2	× 2.205
lb → kg	÷ 2	× 0.454
Kilograms per square centimeter (kg/cm²)		
Pounds per square inch (PSI)		
kg/cm² → PSI	× 14	× 14.223
PSI → kg/cm²	÷ 14	× 0.070
Tonnes (t)		
Short (US) tons (sh t)		
t → sh t	× 1	× 1.102
sh t → t	÷ 1	× 0.907
Ounces troy (oz tr)		
Ounces (oz)		
oz tr → oz	× 1	× 1.097
oz → oz tr	÷ 1	× 0.911

Conversion tables

The tables below can be used to convert units of weight from one measuring system to another. The units included in the tables are troy, US units/UK imperial, and metric.

Grains to Grams		Ounces troy to Grams		Ounces to Grams	
gr	g	oz tr	g	oz	g
1	0.065	1	31.103	1	28.349
2	0.130	2	62.207	2	56.699
3	0.194	3	93.310	3	85.048
4	0.259	4	124.414	4	113.398
5	0.324	5	155.517	5	141.747
6	0.389	6	186.621	6	170.097
7	0.454	7	217.724	7	198.446
8	0.518	8	248.829	8	226.796
9	0.583	9	279.931	9	255.145
10	0.648	10	311.035	10	283.495
20	1.296	20	622.070	20	566.990
30	1.944	30	933.104	30	850.485
40	2.592	40	1,244.139	40	1,133.980
50	3.240	50	1,555.174	50	1,417.475
60	3.888	60	1,866.209	60	1,700.970
70	4.536	70	2,177.243	70	1,984.465
80	5.184	80	2,488.278	80	2,267.960
90	5.832	90	2,799.313	90	2,551.455
100	6.480	100	3,110.348	100	2,834.900

Pounds to Kilograms	
lb	kg
1	0.454
2	0.907
3	1.361
4	1.814
5	2.268
6	2.722
7	3.175
8	3.629
9	4.082
10	4.536
20	9.072
30	13.608
40	18.144
50	22.680
60	27.216
70	31.751
80	36.287
90	40.823
100	45.359

Pounds per square inch to Kilograms per square centimeter	
PSI	kg/cm²
10	0.703
15	1.055
20	1.406
22	1.547
24	1.687
26	1.828
28	1.986
30	2.109
32	2.250
34	2.390
36	2.531
38	2.671
40	2.812
45	3.164
50	3.515

Stones to Kilograms	
st	kg
1	6.350
2	12.700
3	19.050
4	25.401
5	31.751
6	38.101
7	44.452
8	50.802
9	57.152
10	63.502
20	127.006
30	190.509
40	254.012
50	317.515
60	381.018
70	444.521
80	508.023
90	571.526
100	635.029

US units/UK imperial and metric units of weight (continued)

Short (US) tons to Tonnes		Long (UK) tons to Tonnes		Grams to Grains	
sh t	**t**	**l t**	**t**	**g**	**gr**
1	0.907	1	1.016	1	15.432
2	1.814	2	2.032	2	30.865
3	2.721	3	3.048	3	46.297
4	3.628	4	4.064	4	61.729
5	4.535	5	5.080	5	77.162
6	5.443	6	6.096	6	92.594
7	6.350	7	7.112	7	108.027
8	7.257	8	8.128	8	123.459
9	8.164	9	9.144	9	138.891
10	9.071	10	10.160	10	154.324
20	18.143	20	20.320	20	308.647
30	27.215	30	30.481	30	462.971
40	36.287	40	40.641	40	617.294
50	45.359	50	50.802	50	771.618
60	54.431	60	60.962	60	925.942
70	63.502	70	71.123	70	1,080.265
80	72.574	80	81.283	80	1,234.589
90	81.646	90	91.444	90	1,388.912
100	90.718	100	101.604	100	1,543.236

Grams to Ounces troy		Grams to Ounces		Kilograms to Pounds	
g	oz tr	g	oz	kg	lb
1	0.032	1	0.035	1	2.205
2	0.064	2	0.071	2	4.409
3	0.096	3	0.106	3	6.614
4	0.129	4	0.141	4	8.818
5	0.161	5	0.176	5	11.023
6	0.193	6	0.212	6	13.228
7	0.225	7	0.247	7	15.432
8	0.257	8	0.282	8	17.637
9	0.289	9	0.317	9	19.842
10	0.322	10	0.353	10	22.046
20	0.643	20	0.705	20	44.092
30	0.965	30	1.058	30	66.139
40	1.286	40	1.411	40	88.185
50	1.608	50	1.764	50	110.231
60	1.929	60	2.116	60	132.277
70	2.251	70	2.469	70	154.324
80	2.572	80	2.822	80	176.370
90	2.894	90	3.175	90	198.416
100	3.215	100	3.527	100	220.462

US units/UK imperial and metric units of weight (continued)

Kilograms per square centimeter to Pounds per square inch		Tonnes to Short (US) tons		Kilograms to Stones	
kg/cm²	PSI	t	sh t	kg	st
0.6	8.534	1	1.102	1	0.157
0.8	11.378	2	2.205	2	0.315
1.0	14.223	3	3.307	3	0.472
1.2	17.068	4	4.409	4	0.630
1.4	19.912	5	5.512	5	0.787
1.6	22.757	6	6.614	6	0.945
1.8	25.601	7	7.716	7	1.102
2.0	28.446	8	8.818	8	1.260
2.2	31.291	9	9.921	9	1.417
2.4	34.135	10	11.023	10	1.574
2.6	36.980	20	22.046	20	3.149
2.8	39.824	30	33.069	30	4.724
3.0	42.669	40	44.092	40	6.299
3.2	45.514	50	55.116	50	7.874
3.5	49.781	60	66.139	60	9.448
		70	77.162	70	11.023
		80	88.185	80	12.598
		90	99.208	90	14.173
		100	110.231	100	15.747

Tonnes to Long (UK) tons		Ounces troy to Ounces		Ounces to Ounces troy	
t	l t	oz tr	oz	oz	oz tr
1	0.984	1	1.097	1	0.911
2	1.968	2	2.194	2	1.823
3	2.953	3	3.291	3	2.734
4	3.937	4	4.389	4	3.646
5	4.921	5	5.486	5	4.557
6	5.905	6	6.583	6	5.468
7	6.889	7	7.680	7	6.380
8	7.874	8	8.777	8	7.291
9	8.858	9	9.874	9	8.203
10	9.842	10	10.971	10	9.114
20	19.684	20	21.943	20	18.229
30	29.526	30	32.914	30	27.344
40	39.368	40	43.886	40	36.458
50	49.211	50	54.857	50	45.573
60	59.052	60	65.828	60	54.687
70	68.894	70	76.800	70	63.802
80	78.737	80	87.771	80	72.917
90	88.579	90	98.743	90	82.031
100	98.421	100	109.714	100	91.146

Periodic table

The periodic table is a means of classifying and comparing chemical elements. Substances as different as hydrogen, calcium, and gold are all elements; each has distinctive properties and cannot be split chemically into a simpler form.

The table groups elements into seven rows or periods. Elements in the vertical columns, or groups, have similar properties. For example, the first element in any period (called an alkali metal) is reactive; while the last element (a noble, or inert, gas) is almost totally nonreactive.

1 H								
3 Li	4 Be							
11 Na	12 Mg							
19 K	20 Ca	21 Sc	22 Ti	23 V	24 Cr	25 Mn	26 Fe	27 Co
37 Rb	38 Sr	39 Y	40 Zr	41 Nb	42 Mo	43 Tc	44 Ru	45 Rh
55 Cs	56 Ba	57-71 -	72 Hf	73 Ta	74 W	75 Re	76 Os	77 Ir
87 Fr	88 Ra	89-103 -	104 Unq	105 Unp	106 Unh	107 Uns	108 Uno	109 Une

57 La	58 Ce	59 Pr	60 Nd	61 Pm	62 Sm	63 Eu
89 Ac	90 Th	91 Pa	92 U	93 Np	94 Pu	95 Am

The elements are listed in the table in order of their atomic numbers, from 1 to 109 (appearing in the upper left-hand corner of each box). The atomic number represents the number of protons the element has in its nucleus.

The two bottom rows are the lanthanides (57–71) and the actinides (89–103). These are separate because they have such similar properties that they fit the space of only two elements in the main table.

							2 He
		5 B	6 C	7 N	8 O	9 F	10 Ne
		13 Al	14 Si	15 P	16 S	17 Cl	18 Ar
28 Ni	29 Cu	30 Zn	31 Ga	32 Ge	33 As	34 Se	35 Br	36 Kr
46 Pd	47 Ag	48 Cd	49 In	50 Sn	51 Sb	52 Te	53 I	54 Xe
78 Pt	79 Au	80 Hg	81 Tl	82 Pb	83 Bi	84 Po	85 At	86 Rn

64 Gd	65 Tb	66 Dy	67 Ho	68 Er	69 Tm	70 Yb	71 Lu
96 Cm	97 Bk	98 Cf	99 Es	100 Fm	101 Md	102 No	103 Lr

Chemical elements

On the following pages, the elements are listed in three
separate ways: **1** by atomic number; **2** by element
name; and **3** by letter symbol. Each listing includes the
atomic number, element name, symbol, and atomic
weight (or relative atomic mass) of each element.
* Indicates atomic weight of the isotope with the
longest known half-life.

1 BY ATOMIC NUMBER

Atomic No.	Name	Symbol	Atomic weight
1	Hydrogen	H	1.0079
2	Helium	He	4.0026
3	Lithium	Li	6.941
4	Beryllium	Be	9.01218
5	Boron	B	10.81
6	Carbon	C	12.011
7	Nitrogen	N	14.0067
8	Oxygen	O	15.9994
9	Fluorine	F	18.9984
10	Neon	Ne	20.179
11	Sodium	Na	22.98977
12	Magnesium	Mg	24.305
13	Aluminum	Al	26.98154
14	Silicon	Si	28.0855
15	Phosphorus	P	30.97376
16	Sulfur	S	32.064
17	Chlorine	Cl	35.453
18	Argon	Ar	39.948
19	Potassium	K	39.0983
20	Calcium	Ca	40.08

Atomic No.	Name	Symbol	Atomic weight
21	Scandium	Sc	44.9559
22	Titanium	Ti	47.9
23	Vanadium	V	50.9414
24	Chromium	Cr	51.996
25	Manganese	Mn	54.938
26	Iron	Fe	55.847
27	Cobalt	Co	58.9332
28	Nickel	Ni	58.71
29	Copper	Cu	63.546
30	Zinc	Zn	65.381
31	Gallium	Ga	69.72
32	Germanium	Ge	72.59
33	Arsenic	As	74.9216
34	Selenium	Se	78.96
35	Bromine	Br	79.904
36	Krypton	Kr	83.8
37	Rubidium	Rb	85.4678
38	Strontium	Sr	87.62
39	Yttrium	Y	88.9059
40	Zirconium	Zr	91.22
41	Niobium	Nb	92.9064
42	Molybdenum	Mo	95.94
43	Technetium	Tc	96.9064*
44	Ruthenium	Ru	101.07
45	Rhodium	Rh	102.9055
46	Palladium	Pd	106.4
47	Silver	Ag	107.868
48	Cadmium	Cd	112.41
49	Indium	In	114.82

Atomic No.	Name	Symbol	Atomic weight
50	Tin	Sn	118.69
51	Antimony	Sb	121.75
52	Tellurium	Te	127.6
53	Iodine	I	126.905
54	Xenon	Xe	131.3
55	Cesium	Cs	132.9054
56	Barium	Ba	137.33
57	Lanthanum	La	138.9055
58	Caerium	Ce	140.12
59	Praseodymium	Pr	140.9077
60	Neodymium	Nd	144.24
61	Promethium	Pm	144.9128*
62	Samarium	Sm	150.35
63	Europium	Eu	151.96
64	Gadolinium	Gd	157.25
65	Terbium	Tb	158.9254
66	Dysprosium	Dy	162.5
67	Holmium	Ho	164.9304
68	Erbium	Er	167.26
69	Thulium	Tm	168.9342
70	Ytterbium	Yb	173.04
71	Lutetium	Lu	174.97
72	Hafnium	Hf	178.49
73	Tantalum	Ta	180.9479
74	Tungsten	W	183.85
75	Rhenium	Re	186.207
76	Osmium	Os	190.2
77	Iridium	Ir	192.22
78	Platinum	Pt	195.09

Atomic

No.	Name	Symbol	Atomic weight
79	Gold	Au	196.9665
80	Mercury	Hg	200.59
81	Thallium	Tl	204.37
82	Lead	Pb	207.19
83	Bismuth	Bi	208.9804
84	Polonium	Po	208.9824*
85	Astatine	At	209.9870*
86	Radon	Rn	222.017 6*
87	Francium	Fr	223.0197*
88	Radium	Ra	226.0254*
89	Actinium	Ac	227.0278*
90	Thorium	Th	232.0381
91	Protoactinium	Pa	231.0359
92	Uranium	U	238.029*
93	Neptunium	Np	237.0482*
94	Plutonium	Pu	244.0642*
95	Americium	Am	243.0614*
96	Curium	Cm	247.0703*
97	Berkelium	Bk	247.0703*
98	Californium	Cf	251.0796*
99	Einsteinium	Es	254.0880*
100	Fermium	Fm	257.0951*
101	Mendelevium	Md	258.099*
102	Nobelium	No	259.101*
103	Lawrencium	Lr	260.105*
104	Unnilquadium	Unq	261.109*
105	Unnilpentium	Unp	262.114*
106	Unnilhexium	Unh	263.120*
107	Unnilseptium	Uns	262*

Atomic

No.	Name	Symbol	Atomic weight
108	Unniloctium	Uno	265
109	Unnilennium	Une	266*

2 BY ELEMENT NAME

Name	Atomic No.	Symbol	Atomic weight
Actinium	89	Ac	227.0278*
Aluminum	13	Al	26.98154
Americium	95	Am	243.0614*
Antimony	51	Sb	121.75
Argon	18	Ar	39.948
Arsenic	33	As	74.9216
Astatine	85	At	209.9870*
Barium	56	Ba	137.33
Berkelium	97	Bk	247.0703*
Beryllium	4	Be	9.01218
Bismuth	83	Bi	208.9804
Boron	5	B	10.81
Bromine	35	Br	79.904
Cadmium	48	Cd	112.41
Calcium	20	Ca	40.08
Californium	98	Cf	251.0796*
Carbon	6	C	12.011
Cerium	58	Ce	140.12
Cesium	55	Cs	132.9054
Chlorine	17	Cl	35.453
Chromium	24	Cr	51.996
Cobalt	27	Co	58.9332

Name	Atomic No.	Symbol	Atomic weight
Copper	29	Cu	63.546
Curium	96	Cm	247.703*
Dysprosium	66	Dy	162.5
Einsteinium	99	Es	254.0880*
Erbium	68	Er	167.26
Europium	63	Eu	151.96
Fermium	100	Fm	257.0951*
Fluorine	9	F	18.9984
Francium	87	Fr	223.0197*
Gadolinium	64	Gd	157.25
Gallium	31	Ga	69.72
Germanium	32	Ge	72.59
Gold	79	Au	196.9665
Hafnium	72	Hf	178.49
Helium	2	He	4.0026
Holmium	67	Ho	164.9304
Hydrogen	1	H	1.0079
Indium	49	In	114.82
Iodine	53	I	126.9045
Iridium	77	Ir	192.22
Iron	26	Fe	55.847
Krypton	36	Kr	83.8
Lanthanum	57	La	138.9055
Lawrencium	103	Lr	260.105*
Lead	82	Pb	207.19
Lithium	3	Li	6.941
Lutetium	71	Lu	174.97
Magnesium	12	Mg	24.305

Name	Atomic No.	Symbol	Atomic weight
Manganese	25	Mn	54.938
Mendelevium	101	Md	258.099*
Mercury	80	Hg	200.59
Molybdenum	42	Mo	95.94
Neodymium	60	Nd	144.24
Neon	10	Ne	20.179
Neptunium	93	Np	237.0482*
Nickel	28	Ni	58.71
Niobium	41	Nb	92.9064
Nitrogen	7	N	14.0067
Nobelium	102	No	259.101*
Osmium	76	Os	190.2
Oxygen	8	O	15.9994
Palladium	46	Pd	106.4
Phosphorus	15	P	30.97376
Platinum	78	Pt	195.09
Plutonium	94	Pu	244.0642*
Polonium	84	Po	208.9824*
Potassium	19	K	39.0983
Praseodymium	59	Pr	140.9077
Promethium	61	Pm	144.9128*
Protoactinium	91	Pa	231.0359
Radium	88	Ra	226.0254*
Radon	86	Rn	222.0176*
Rhenium	75	Re	186.207
Rhodium	45	Rh	102.9055
Rubidium	37	Rb	85.4678
Ruthenium	44	Ru	101.07
Samarium	62	Sm	150.35

Name	Atomic No.	Symbol	Atomic weight
Scandium	21	Sc	44.9559
Selenium	34	Se	78.96
Silicon	14	Si	28.0855
Silver	47	Ag	107.868
Sodium	11	Na	22.98977
Strontium	38	Sr	87.62
Sulfur	16	S	32.064
Tantalum	73	Ta	180.9479
Technetium	43	Tc	96.9064*
Tellurium	52	Te	127.6
Terbium	65	Tb	158.9254
Thallium	81	Tl	204.37
Thorium	90	Th	232.0381
Thulium	69	Tm	168.9342
Tin	50	Sn	118.69
Titanium	22	Ti	47.9
Tungsten	74	W	183.85
Unnilennium	109	Une	266*
Unnilhexium	106	Unh	263.120*
Unniloctium	108	Uno	265
Unnilpentium	105	Unp	262.114*
Unnilquadium	104	Unq	261.109*
Unnilseptium	107	Uns	262*
Uranium	92	U	238.029*
Vanadium	23	V	50.9414
Xenon	54	Xe	131.3
Ytterbium	70	Yb	173.04
Yttrium	39	Y	88.9059

	Atomic		
Name	No.	Symbol	Atomic weight
Zinc	30	Zn	65.381
Zirconium	40	Zr	91.22

3 BY LETTER SYMBOL

Symbol	**Atomic** No.	Name	Atomic weight
Ac	89	Actinium	227.0278*
Ag	47	Silver	107.868
Al	13	Aluminum	26.98154
Am	95	Americium	243.0614*
Ar	18	Argon	39.948
As	33	Arsenic	74.9216
At	85	Astatine	209.9870*
Au	79	Gold	196.9665
B	5	Boron	10.81
Ba	56	Barium	137.33
Be	4	Beryllium	9.01218
Bk	97	Berkelium	247.0703*
Bi	83	Bismuth	208.9804
Br	35	Bromine	79.904
C	6	Carbon	12.011
Ca	20	Calcium	40.08
Cd	48	Cadmium	112.41
Ce	58	Cerium	140.12
Cf	98	Californium	251.0796*
Cl	17	Chlorine	35.453
Cm	96	Curium	247.0703*
Co	27	Cobalt	58.9332
Cr	24	Chromium	51.996

Symbol	Atomic No.	Name	Atomic weight
Cs	55	Cesium	132.9054
Cu	29	Copper	63.546
Dy	66	Dysprosium	162.5
Er	68	Erbium	167.26
Es	99	Einsteinium	254.088*
Eu	63	Europium	151.96
F	9	Fluorine	18.9984
Fe	26	Iron	55.847
Fm	100	Fermium	257.0951*
Fr	87	Francium	223.0197*
Ga	31	Gallium	69.72
Gd	64	Gadolinium	157.25
Ge	32	Germanium	72.59
H	1	Hydrogen	1.0079
He	2	Helium	4.0026
Hf	72	Hafnium	178.49
Hg	80	Mercury	200.59
Ho	67	Holmium	164.9304
I	53	Iodine	126.9045
In	49	Indium	114.82
Ir	77	Iridium	192.22
K	19	Potassium	39.0983
Kr	36	Krypton	83.8
La	57	Lanthanum	138.9055
Li	3	Lithium	6.941
Lr	103	Lawrencium	260.105*
Lu	71	Lutetium	174.97
Md	101	Mendelevium	258.099*
Mg	12	Magnesium	24.305

Symbol	Atomic No.	Name	Atomic weight
Mn	25	Manganese	54.938
Mo	42	Molybdenum	95.94
N	7	Nitrogen	14.0067
Na	11	Sodium	22.98977
Nb	41	Niobium	92.9064
Nd	60	Neodymium	144.24
Ne	10	Neon	20.179
Ni	28	Nickel	58.71
No	102	Nobelium	259.101*
Np	93	Neptunium	237.0482*
O	8	Oxygen	15.9994
Os	76	Osmium	190.2
P	15	Phosphorus	30.97376
Pa	91	Protoactinium	231.0359
Pb	82	Lead	207.19
Pd	46	Palladium	106.4
Pm	61	Promethium	144.9128*
Po	84	Polonium	208.9824*
Pr	59	Praseodymium	140.9077
Pt	78	Platinum	195.09
Pu	94	Plutonium	244.0642*
Ra	88	Radium	226.0254*
Rb	37	Rubidium	85.4678
Re	75	Rhenium	186.207
Rh	45	Rhodium	102.9055
Rn	86	Radon	222.0176*
Ru	44	Ruthenium	101.07
S	16	Sulfur	32.064
Sb	51	Antimony	121.75

Symbol	Atomic No.	Name	Atomic weight
Sc	21	Scandium	44.9559
Se	34	Selenium	78.96
Si	14	Silicon	28.0855
Sm	62	Samarium	150.35
Sn	50	Tin	118.69
Sr	38	Strontium	87.62
Ta	73	Tantalum	180.9479
Tb	65	Terbium	158.9254
Tc	43	Technetium	96.9064*
Te	52	Tellurium	127.6
Th	90	Thorium	232.0381
Ti	22	Titanium	47.9
Tl	81	Thallium	204.37
Tm	69	Thulium	168.9342
U	92	Uranium	238.029*
Une	109	Unnilennium	266*
Unh	106	Unnilhexium	263.120*
Uno	108	Unniloctium	265
Unp	105	Unnilpentium	262.114*
Unq	104	Unnilquadium	261.109*
Uns	107	Unnilseptium	262*
V	23	Vanadium	50.9414
W	74	Tungsten	183.85
Xe	54	Xenon	131.3
Y	39	Yttrium	88.9059
Yb	70	Ytterbium	173.04
Zn	30	Zinc	65.381
Zr	40	Zirconium	91.22

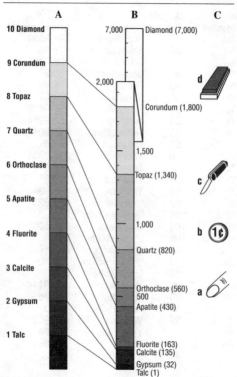

A   B   C

10 Diamond   7,000 ⌐ Diamond (7,000)

9 Corundum   2,000 ⌐   d

8 Topaz   Corundum (1,800)

7 Quartz   1,500 ⌐

6 Orthoclase   Topaz (1,340)   c

5 Apatite   1,000 ⌐

4 Fluorite   Quartz (820)   b 1¢

3 Calcite   Orthoclase (560)
                        500 ⌐   a
2 Gypsum   Apatite (430)

1 Talc   Fluorite (163)
                               Calcite (135)
                               Gypsum (32)
                               Talc (1)

Scales of hardness

Solids vary in their degree of hardness, which indicates their resistance to being scratched or cut.

A Mohs' scale

Mohs' scale is used to measure the relative hardness of minerals. The framework uses the 10 minerals – talc to diamond – shown in the scale. Each of these minerals is assigned a numerical value from 1 to 10: the higher the number, the harder the mineral.

Order is determined by the ability of a mineral to scratch all those that have a lower number and to be scratched by those with a higher number. Once this is established, it is possible to place all other minerals on the scale by means of the same scratching procedure.

B Knoop scale

Another system of measuring the hardness of minerals is the Knoop scale. The Knoop scale gives absolute rather than relative measurements. Readings on this scale are made by measuring the size of the indentation made by a diamond-shaped device dropped on the material.

Again, the higher the number the harder the substance, but the intervals between minerals and levels of hardness differ greatly from scale to scale. Minerals with values between 1 and 7 on Mohs' scale fall below 1,000 on the Knoop scale, and between 8 and 9 fall below 2,000, but diamond falls at 7,000.

C Common-object scale

A simple way of measuring hardness uses common objects, whose hardness on the Mohs' scale is known:

a) fingernail (2–2.5 Mohs')   c) knife blade (5–6)

b) coin (4)   d) knife sharpener (8–9)

5: Energy

Formulas

Below are listed the multiplication/division factors for
converting units of energy from one measuring system
to another. Note that two kinds of factors are given:
quick, for an approximate conversion that can be made
without a calculator; and accurate, for an exact
conversion.

	Kilowatts (kW) Horsepower (hp)	**Quick**	**Accurate**
	kW ⟶ hp	× 1.5	× 1.341
	hp ⟶ kW	÷ 1.5	× 0.746
	Calories (cal) Joules (J)		
	cal ⟶ J	× 4	× 4.187
	J ⟶ cal	÷ 4	× 0.239
	Kilocalories (kcal) Kilojoules (kJ)		
	kcal ⟶ kJ	× 4	× 4.187
	kJ ⟶ kcal	÷ 4	× 0.239

Conversion tables
The tables below can be used to convert units of energy from one measuring system to another.

Horsepower to Kilowatts		Kilowatts to Horsepower	
hp	kW	kW	hp
1	0.746	1	1.341
2	1.491	2	2.682
3	2.237	3	4.023
4	2.983	4	5.364
5	3.729	5	6.705
6	4.474	6	8.046
7	5.220	7	9.387
8	5.966	8	10.728
9	6.711	9	12.069
10	7.457	10	13.410
20	14.914	20	26.820
30	22.371	30	40.231
40	29.828	40	53.641
50	37.285	50	67.051
60	44.742	60	80.461
70	52.199	70	93.871
80	59.656	80	107.280
90	67.113	90	120.690
100	74.570	100	134.100

Metric units of energy

Joules to Calories international		Kilojoules to Kilocalories international	
J	cal	kJ	kcal
1	0.239	1	0.239
2	0.478	2	0.478
3	0.716	3	0.716
4	0.955	4	0.955
5	1.194	5	1.194
6	1.433	6	1.433
7	1.672	7	1.672
8	1.911	8	1.911
9	2.150	9	2.150
10	2.388	10	2.388
20	4.777	20	4.777
30	7.165	30	7.165
40	9.554	40	9.554
50	11.942	50	11.942
60	14.330	60	14.330
70	16.719	70	16.719
80	19.108	80	19.108
90	21.496	90	21.496
100	23.885	100	23.885

Calories international to Joules	
cal	J
1	4.187
2	8.374
3	12.560
4	16.747
5	20.934
6	25.121
7	29.308
8	33.494
9	37.681
10	41.868
20	83.736
30	125.604
40	167.472
50	209.340
60	251.208
70	293.076
80	334.944
90	376.812
100	418.680

Kilocalories international to Kilojoules	
kcal	kJ
1	4.187
2	8.374
3	12.560
4	16.747
5	20.934
6	25.121
7	29.308
8	33.494
9	37.681
10	41.868
20	83.736
30	125.604
40	167.472
50	209.340
60	251.208
70	293.076
80	334.944
90	376.812
100	418.680

Electromagnetic spectrum

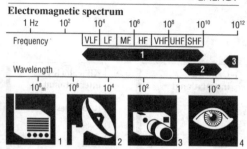

Measuring energy

Light and radio waves, X-rays, and other forms of
energy are transmitted through space as
electromagnetic waves. These waves have alternating
high and low points – crests and troughs – like actual
waves. The distance between wave crests is called the
wavelength; this is measured in meters. Frequency
refers to the number of waves per second passing a
certain point; this is measured in hertz (Hz).

Above is an electromagnetic spectrum, showing the
different forms of energy in order of frequency and
wavelength. The top part of the diagram shows the
frequency in hertz; the lower part measures the
wavelength in meters.

1 Radio waves

These waves transmit television and radio signals. This
section of the spectrum is divided into bands, from
VLF (very low frequency) – used for time signals – to
SHF (super-high frequency) – used for space and
satellite communication.

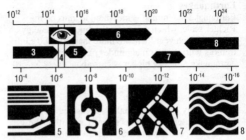

2 Radar and microwaves
Radar bounces waves off objects, allowing unseen objects to be seen; microwaves can cook food quickly.
3 Infrared waves
These waves are emitted by all hot objects.
4 Visible light
The band of visible light from red to violet.
5 Ultraviolet light
In small amounts, these waves produce vitamin D and cause skin to tan; in larger amounts they can damage living cells.
6 X-rays
Used to photograph the internal structures of the body.
7 Gamma rays
Emitted during the decay of some radioisotopes, these waves can be very damaging to the body.
8 Cosmic rays
Caused by nuclear explosions and reactions in space, nearly all of these waves are absorbed by the Earth's atmosphere.

Earthquakes

Earthquake magnitude is measured in units on the
Richter scale, which measures the amount of energy
released. Each year there are more than 300,000 earth
tremors with Richter magnitudes of 2 to 2.9. An
earthquake of 8.5 or higher occurs about every 5 to 10
years.

Intensity

The intensity of an earthquake is measured on the
Mercalli scale; the numbers refer to an earthquake's
effect at a specific place on the Earth's surface.

Below are listed numbers on the Mercalli scale and
the characteristics of each.

No.	Characteristic
I	instrumental (detected only by seismograph)
II	feeble (noticed only by people at rest)
III	slight (similar to vibrations from a passing truck)
IV	moderate (felt indoors, parked cars rock)
V	rather strong (felt generally, waking sleepers)
VI	strong (trees sway, some damage)
VII	very strong (general alarm, walls crack)
VIII	destructive (walls collapse)
IX	ruinous (some houses collapse, ground cracks)
X	disastrous (buildings destroyed, rails bend)
XI	very disastrous (landslides, few buildings survive)
XII	catastrophic (total destruction)

Listed below are the Mercalli and Richter scales, with equivalents in joules, and a table comparing the Richter scale with joules.

Mercalli	Richter	Joules	Richter	Joules
I	<3.5	$<1.6 \times 10^7$ J	0	6.3×10^{-2} J
II	3.5	1.6×10^7 J	1	1.6×10 J
III	4.2	7.5×10^8 J	2	4.0×10^3 J
IV	4.5	4.0×10^9 J	3	1.0×10^6 J
V	4.8	2.1×10^{10} J	4	2.5×10^8 J
VI	5.4	5.7×10^{11} J	5	6.3×10^{10} J
VII	6.1	2.8×10^{13} J	6	1.6×10^{13} J
VIII	6.5	2.5×10^{14} J	7	4.0×10^{15} J
IX	6.9	2.3×10^{15} J	8	1.0×10^{18} J
X	7.3	2.1×10^{16} J	9	2.5×10^{20} J
XI	8.1	1.7×10^{18} J	10	6.3×10^{22} J
XII	>8.1	$>1.7 \times 10^{18}$ J		

Actual earthquakes

The table below lists the year of selected earthquakes in different parts of the world and where they occurred, as well as the Richter magnitude of each.

Earthquakes	Richter
Assam, India (1897)	8.7
Alaska, USA (1964)	8.6
Concepción, Chile (1960)	8.5
San Francisco, USA (1906)	8.25
Mexico City, Mexico (1985)	8.1
Guatemala (1976)	7.9
Tangshan, China (1976)	7.6
Messina, Italy (1908)	7.5
Vrancea, Romania (1977)	7.2
San Francisco, USA (1989)	6.9

Decibels

The loudness of a sound is measured by the size of its vibrations; this is measured in decibels (dB).

Decibel scale

The dB scale is relative and increases exponentially, beginning with the smallest sound change that can be heard by humans (0–1 dB). A 20 dB sound is 10 times louder than a 10 dB sound; a 30 dB sound is 100 times as loud as that. Noises at the level of 120–130 dB can cause pain in humans; higher levels can cause permanent ear damage. The dB ratings (at certain distances) of some common noises are listed on page 135.

Wave amplitude

Amplitude (**a**) is the distance between a wave peak or trough and an intermediate line of equilibrium. The greater the amount of energy transmitted in a sound wave, the greater is the wave's amplitude and the louder the sound heard.

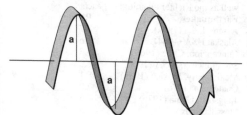

A	0 dB	human minimum audibility
B	30 dB	soft whisper at 15 ft
C	50 dB	inside urban home
D	55 dB	light traffic at 50 ft
E	60 dB	conversation at 3 ft
F	85 dB	pneumatic drill at 50 ft
G	90 dB	heavy traffic at 50 ft
H	100 dB	loud shout at 50 ft
I	105 dB	airplane take-off at 2,000 ft
J	117 dB	inside full-volume disco
K	120 dB	airplane take-off at 200 ft
L	130 dB	pain threshold for humans
M	140 dB	airplane take-off at 100 ft

Energy needs by activity

	Activity	☐ Women	■ Men
A	Sleeping	230 kJ; 55 kcal	272 kJ; 65 kcal
B	Sitting	293 kJ; 70 kcal	377 kJ; 90 kcal
C	Standing	419 kJ; 100 kcal	502 kJ; 120 kcal
D	Walking	754 kJ; 180 kcal	921 kJ; 220 kcal
E	Walking (uphill)	1,507 kJ; 360 kcal	1,842 kJ; 440 kcal
F	Running	1,759 kJ; 420 kcal	2,512 kJ; 600 kcal

Kilojoules (kJ) per hour

| 0 | 500 | 1,000 | 1,500 | 2,000 | 2,500 |

A
B
C
D
E
F

| 0 | 100 | 200 | 300 | 400 | 500 | 600 |

Kilocalories (kcal) per hour

Men use more kilocalories than women for all activities because men have more weight to carry around, and because women usually have more body fat and so need less energy to retain body heat.

Energy values of selected foods

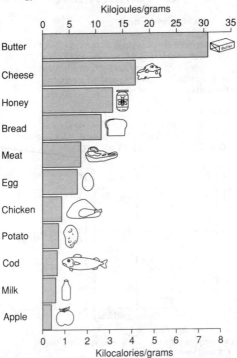

6: Temperature

Systems of measurement

Below, the different systems of temperature
measurement are compared: Fahrenheit (°F), Celsius
(°C), Réaumur (°r), Rankine (°R), and Kelvin (K).
Also listed are the formulas for converting temperature
measurements from one system to another.

Formulas

°F ➡ °C	(°F−32)÷1.8	°r ➡ K	(°r×1.25)+273.16
°C ➡ °F	(°C×1.8)+32	°R ➡ K	°R÷1.8
°F ➡ K	(°F+459.67)÷1.8	K ➡ °F	(K×1.8)−459.67
°C ➡ K	°C+273.16	K ➡ °C	K−273.16

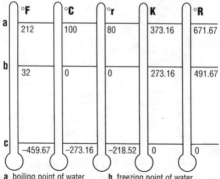

	°F	°C	°r	K	°R
a	212	100	80	373.16	671.67
b	32	0	0	273.16	491.67
c	−459.67	−273.16	−218.52	0	0

a boiling point of water   **b** freezing point of water
c absolute zero

Conversion tables

The tables below list the equivalent units of temperature in the Fahrenheit, Celsius, and Kelvin systems.

Fahrenheit to Celsius to Kelvin			Fahrenheit to Celsius to Kelvin		
°F	°C	K	°F	°C	K
−40.0	−40	233	−4.0	−20	253
−38.2	−39	234	−2.2	−19	254
−36.4	−38	235	−0.4	−18	255
−34.6	−37	236	1.4	−17	256
−32.8	−36	237	3.2	−16	257
−31.0	−35	238	5.0	−15	258
−29.2	−34	239	6.8	−14	259
−27.4	−33	240	8.6	−13	260
−25.6	−32	241	10.4	−12	261
−23.8	−31	242	12.2	−11	262
−22.0	−30	243	14.0	−10	263
−20.2	−29	244	15.8	−9	264
−18.4	−28	245	17.6	−8	265
−16.6	−27	246	19.4	−7	266
−14.8	−26	247	21.2	−6	267
−13.0	−25	248	23.0	−5	268
−11.2	−24	249	24.8	−4	269
−9.4	−23	250	26.6	−3	270
−7.6	−22	251	28.4	−2	271
−5.8	−21	252	30.2	−1	272

Fahrenheit, Celsius, and Kelvin unit equivalents (continued)

Fahrenheit to Celsius to Kelvin		
°F	°C	K
32.0	0	273
33.8	1	274
35.6	2	275
37.4	3	276
39.2	4	277
41.0	5	278
42.8	6	279
44.6	7	280
46.4	8	281
48.2	9	282
50.0	10	283
51.8	11	284
53.6	12	285
55.4	13	286
57.2	14	287
59.0	15	288
60.8	16	289
62.6	17	290
64.4	18	291
66.2	19	292

Fahrenheit to Celsius to Kelvin		
°F	°C	K
68.0	20	293
69.8	21	294
71.6	22	295
73.4	23	296
75.2	24	297
77.0	25	298
78.8	26	299
80.6	27	300
82.4	28	301
84.2	29	302
86.0	30	303
87.8	31	304
89.6	32	305
91.4	33	306
93.2	34	307
95.0	35	308
96.8	36	309
98.6	37	310
100.4	38	311
102.2	39	312

°F	°C	K
Fahrenheit to Celsius to Kelvin		
104.0	40	313
105.8	41	314
107.6	42	315
109.4	43	316
111.2	44	317
113.0	45	318
114.8	46	319
116.6	47	320
118.4	48	321
120.2	49	322
122.0	50	323
123.8	51	324
125.6	52	325
127.4	53	326
129.2	54	327
131.0	55	328
132.8	56	329
134.6	57	330
136.4	58	331
138.2	59	332

°F	°C	K
Fahrenheit to Celsius to Kelvin		
140.0	60	333
141.8	61	334
143.6	62	335
145.4	63	336
147.2	64	337
149.0	65	338
150.8	66	339
152.6	67	340
154.4	68	341
156.2	69	342
158.0	70	343
159.8	71	344
161.6	72	345
163.4	73	346
165.2	74	347
167.0	75	348
168.8	76	349
170.6	77	350
172.4	78	351
174.2	79	352

Fahrenheit, Celsius, and Kelvin unit equivalents (continued)

Fahrenheit to Celsius to Kelvin				Fahrenheit to Celsius to Kelvin		
°F	°C	K		°F	°C	K
176.0	80	353		212.0	100	373
177.8	81	354		213.8	101	374
179.6	82	355		215.6	102	375
181.4	83	356		217.4	103	376
183.2	84	357		219.2	104	377
185.0	85	358		221.0	105	378
186.8	86	359		222.8	106	379
188.6	87	360		224.6	107	380
190.4	88	361		226.4	108	381
192.2	89	362		228.2	109	382
194.0	90	363		230.0	110	383
195.8	91	364		231.8	111	384
197.6	92	365		233.6	112	385
199.4	93	366		235.4	113	386
201.2	94	367		237.2	114	387
203.0	95	368		239.0	115	388
204.8	96	369		240.8	116	389
206.6	97	370		242.6	117	390
208.4	98	371		244.4	118	391
210.2	99	372		246.2	119	392

Useful temperatures

Quick temperature reference

Condition	°F	°C
Water freezes	32	0
Mild winter day	50	10
Warm spring day	68	20
Hot summer day	86	30
Body temperature	98.6	37
Heat wave	104	40
Water boils	212	100

Oven temperatures

Below is a table of Fahrenheit/Celsius conversions for common oven temperatures.

°F	°C	Oven
225	110	very cool
250	130	
275	140	cool
300	150	
325	170	moderate
350	180	
375	190	moderately hot
400	200	
425	220	hot
450	230	
475	240	very hot

For other conversions, use the following formulas:
°F to °C Subtract 32, then divide by 1.8.
°C to °F Multiply by 1.8, then add 32.

7: Time

Units of time

Listed below are the names of time periods that are artificially derived, as opposed to astronomical periods.

Time periods

Below are some widely used names for periods of time.

Name	Period	Name	Period
millennium	1,000 years	leap year	366 days
half-millennium	500 years	year	365 days
century	100 years	year	12 months
half-century	50 years	year	52 weeks
decade	10 years	month	28–31 days
half-decade	5 years	week	7 days

Days, hours, minutes

Below are listed the basic subdivisions of a day and their equivalents.

1 day = 24 hours = 1,440 minutes = 86,400 seconds
1 hour = $\frac{1}{24}$ day = 60 minutes = 3,600 seconds
1 minute = $\frac{1}{1,440}$ day = $\frac{1}{60}$ hour = 60 seconds
1 second = $\frac{1}{86,400}$ day = $\frac{1}{3,600}$ hour = $\frac{1}{60}$ minute

Seconds

Greater precision in measuring time has required seconds (s) to be broken down into smaller units, using standard metric prefixes.

1 terasecond (Ts)	10^{12} s	31,689 years
1 gigasecond (Gs)	10^{9} s	31.7 years
1 megasecond (Ms)	10^{6} s	11.6 days
1 kilosecond (ks)	10^{3} s	16.67 minutes
1 millisecond (ms)	10^{-3} s	0.001 seconds

1 microsecond (μs)	10^{-6} s	0.000001
1 nanosecond (ns)	10^{-9} s	0.000000001
1 picosecond (ps)	10^{-12} s	0.000000000001
1 femtosecond (fs)	10^{-15} s	0.000000000000001
1 attosecond (as)	10^{-18} s	0.000000000000000001

Astronomical time

Time can be measured by motion; in fact, the motion of the Earth, Sun, Moon, and stars provided humans with the first means of measuring time.

Years, months, days

Sidereal times are calculated by the Earth's position according to fixed stars. The anomalistic year is measured according to the Earth's orbit in relation to the perihelion (Earth's minimum distance to the Sun). Tropical times refer to the apparent passage of the Sun and the actual passage of the Moon across the Earth's equatorial plane. The synodic month is based on the phases of the Moon. Solar time (as in a mean solar day) refers to periods of darkness and light averaged over a year.

Time	Days	Hours	Minutes	Seconds
sidereal year	365	6	9	10
anomalistic year	365	6	13	53
tropical year	365	5	48	45
sidereal month	27	7	43	11
tropical month	27	7	43	5
synodic month	29	12	44	3
mean solar day	0	24	0	0
sidereal day	0	23	56	4

Equinox and solstice

The inclination of the Earth to its plane of rotation around the Sun produces variations in the lengths of day and night at different times of the year. Solstices are when the Sun appears to be overhead at midday at the maximum distances north and south of the Equator. At the summer solstice, days are longest and nights are shortest; this is reversed at the winter solstice. Equinoxes are when day and night are equal everywhere; at these times, the Sun appears overhead at midday at the Equator.

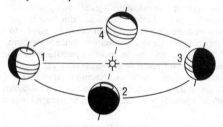

The table lists the dates of the solstices and equinox in each hemisphere, keyed by number to the diagram above, which shows the Earth at four points in its orbit.

Date	Northern	Southern
1 June 21	summer solstice	winter solstice
2 Sept. 23	autumnal equinox	vernal equinox
3 Dec. 22	winter solstice	summer solstice
4 March 21	vernal equinox	autumnal equinox

Years and seasons

Seasonal variations are another result of the inclination of the Earth's axis to its plane of rotation around the Sun. Parts of the globe tilted away from the Sun receive less radiant energy per unit area than those receiving rays more directly. The table below lists the seasonal equivalents in the two hemispheres, keyed by number to the diagram on the previous page.

Northern	Southern
1 summer	winter
2 fall	spring
3 winter	summer
4 spring	fall

Length of days

a Arctic Circle: 66° 33′N – 24 hours daylight
b 49° 3′N – 16 hours daylight
c The Equator: 0° – 12 hours daylight
d 49° 3′S – 8 hours daylight
e Antarctic Circle: 66° 33′S – 0 hours daylight

The diagram above illustrates the variety in the length of the day (21 June) at different latitudes (° = degrees; ′ = minutes). On this day, the northern hemisphere receives the maximum hours of daylight; the southern hemisphere, the minimum.

Geological timescale

Era millions of years ago	Period	Epoch
Cenozoic 65–present	Quaternary 2–present	Holocene 0.01–present
		Pleistocene 2–0.01
	Tertiary 65–2	Pliocene 7–2
		Miocene 26–7
		Oligocene 38–26
		Eocene 54–38
		Paleocene 65–54
Mesozoic 248–65	Cretaceous 136–65	
	Jurassic 193–136	
	Triassic 225–193	
Paleozoic 590–248	Permian 280–225	
	*Carboniferous 345–280	
	Devonian 395–345	
	Silurian 440–395	
	Ordovician 500–440	
	Cambrian 590–500	
Precambrian before 590		

* Mississippian and Pennsylvanian periods in N. America

The zodiac year

Aries
Ram
*(March 21-
April 20)*

Taurus
Bull
*(April 21-
May 20)*

Gemini
Twins
*(May 21-
June 20)*

Cancer
Crab
*(June 21-
July 21)*

Leo
Lion
*(July 22-
August 21)*

Virgo
Virgin
*(August 22-
September 21)*

Libra
Scales
*(Sepember 22-
October 22)*

Scorpio
Scorpion
*(October 23-
November 21)*

Sagittarius
Archer
*(November 22-
December 20)*

Capricorn
Goat
*(December 21-
January 19)*

Aquarius
Water-bearer
*(January 20-
February 18)*

Pisces
Fish
*(February 19-
March 20)*

Types of calendar

The number of days in a year varies among cultures and from year to year.

Gregorian

The Gregorian calendar is a 16th-century adaptation of the Julian calendar devised in the 1st century BC. The year in this calendar is based on the solar year, which lasts about 365 $1/4$ days. In this system, years whose number is not divisible by 4 have 365 days, as do centennial years unless the figures before the zeros are divisible by 4. All other years have 366 days; these are leap years.

   Below are the names of the months and number of days for a non-leap year.

January	31	July	31
February	28*	August	31
March	31	September	30
April	30	October	31
May	31	November	30
June	30	December	31

* 29 in leap years.

Jewish

A year in the Jewish calendar has 13 months if its number, when divided by 9, leaves 0, 3, 6, 8, 11, 14, or 17; otherwise, it has 12 months. The year is based on the lunar year, but its number of months varies to keep broadly in line with the solar cycle. Its precise number of days is fixed with reference to particular festivals that must not fall on certain days of the week.

Below are the names of the months and number of days in each for the year 5471, a 12-month year (1980 AD in Gregorian).

Tishri	30	Nisan	30
Cheshvan	29*	Iyar	29
Kislev	29*	Sivan	30
Tevet	29	Tammuz	29
Shevat	30	Av	30
Adar	29†	Elul	29

* 30 in some years.

† In 13-month years, the month Veadar, with 29 days, falls between Adar and Nisan.

Muslim

A year in the Muslim calendar has 355 days if its number, when divided by 30, leaves 2, 5, 7, 10, 13, 16, 18, 21, 24, 26, or 29; otherwise it has 354 days. As in the Jewish calendar, years are based on the lunar cycle.

Below are the names of the months and number of days in each for the Muslim year 1401 (1980 AD in Gregorian).

Muharram	30	Rajab	30
Safar	29	Sha'ban	29
Rabi'I	30	Ramadan	30
Rabi'II	29	Shawwal	29
Jumada I	30	Dhu l-Qa'dah	30
Jumada II	29	Dhu l-Hijja	30*

* 29 in some years.

Wedding anniversaries

Year	Traditional (alternative)	Modern
1st	Paper (plastics)	Clocks
2nd	Cotton (calico)	China
3rd	Leather	Crystal, glass
4th	Linen (silk, synthetics)	Electrical appliances
5th	Wood	Silverware
6th	Iron	Wood
7th	Wool (copper, brass)	Desk sets
8th	Bronze (electrical appliances)	Linen, lace
9th	Pottery (china)	Leather
10th	Tin (aluminum)	Diamond jewelry
11th	Steel	Fashion jewelry, accessories
12th	Silk (linen)	Pearls or colored gems
13th	Lace	Textile, furs
14th	Ivory	Gold jewelry
15th	Crystal (glass)	Watches
20th	China	Platinum
25th	Silver	Sterling silver jubilee
30th	Pearl	Diamond
35th	Coral (jade)	Jade
40th	Ruby (garnets)	Ruby
45th	Sapphire (tourmalines)	Sapphire
50th	Gold	Gold
55th	Emerald (turquoise)	Emerald
60th	Diamond (gold)	Diamond

Perpetual calendar

How to use the calendar To discover on which day of
the week any date between the years 1780 and 2046
falls, look up the year in the key and the letter shown to
the right will indicate which of the calendars A–N you
should consult.

Key:

1780	N	1805	C	1830	F
1781	B	1806	D	1831	G
1782	C	1807	E	1832	H
1783	D	1808	M	1833	C
1784	L	1809	A	1834	D
1785	G	1810	B	1835	E
1786	A	1811	C	1836	M
1787	B	1812	K	1837	A
1788	J	1813	F	1838	B
1789	E	1814	G	1839	C
1790	F	1815	A	1840	K
1791	G	1816	I	1841	F
1792	H	1817	D	1842	G
1793	C	1818	E	1843	A
1794	D	1819	F	1844	I
1795	E	1820	N	1845	D
1796	M	1821	B	1846	E
1797	A	1822	C	1847	F
1798	B	1823	D	1848	N
1799	C	1824	L	1849	B
1800	D	1825	G	1850	C
1801	E	1826	A	1851	D
1802	F	1827	B	1852	L
1803	G	1828	J	1853	G
1804	H	1829	E	1854	A

1855	B	1887	G	1919	D
1856	J	1888	H	1920	L
1857	E	1889	C	1921	G
1858	F	1890	D	1922	A
1859	G	1891	E	1923	B
1860	H	1892	M	1924	J
1861	C	1893	A	1925	E
1862	D	1894	B	1926	F
1863	E	1895	C	1927	G
1864	M	1896	K	1928	H
1865	A	1897	F	1929	C
1866	B	1898	G	1930	D
1867	C	1899	A	1931	E
1868	K	1900	B	1932	M
1869	F	1901	C	1933	A
1870	G	1902	D	1934	B
1871	A	1903	E	1935	C
1872	I	1904	M	1936	K
1873	D	1905	A	1937	F
1874	E	1906	B	1938	G
1875	F	1907	C	1939	A
1876	N	1908	K	1940	I
1877	B	1909	F	1941	D
1878	C	1910	G	1942	E
1879	D	1911	A	1943	F
1880	L	1912	I	1944	N
1881	G	1913	D	1945	B
1882	A	1914	E	1946	C
1883	B	1915	F	1947	D
1884	J	1916	N	1948	L
1885	E	1917	B	1949	G
1886	F	1918	C	1950	A

1951	B	1983	G	2015	E
1952	J	1984	H	2016	M
1953	E	1985	C	2017	A
1954	F	1986	D	2018	B
1955	G	1987	E	2019	C
1956	H	1988	M	2020	K
1957	C	1989	A	2021	F
1958	D	1990	B	2022	G
1959	E	1991	C	2023	A
1960	M	1992	K	2024	I
1961	A	1993	F	2025	D
1962	B	1994	G	2026	E
1963	C	1995	A	2027	F
1964	K	1996	I	2028	N
1965	F	1997	D	2029	B
1966	G	1998	E	2030	C
1967	A	1999	F	2031	D
1968	I	2000	N	2032	L
1969	D	2001	B	2033	G
1970	E	2002	C	2034	A
1971	F	2003	D	2035	B
1972	N	2004	L	2036	J
1973	B	2005	G	2037	E
1974	C	2006	A	2038	F
1975	D	2007	B	2039	G
1976	L	2008	J	2040	H
1977	G	2009	E	2041	C
1978	A	2010	F	2042	D
1979	B	2011	G	2043	E
1980	J	2012	H	2044	M
1981	E	2013	C	2045	A
1982	F	2014	D	2046	B

A 1786 1797 1809 1815 1826 1837 1843
       1854 1865 1871 1882 1893 1899 1905

JANUARY
S	M	T	W	T	F	S
	1	2	3	4	5	6	7
8	9	10	11	12	13	14
15	16	17	18	19	20	21
22	23	24	25	26	27	28
29	30	31				

FEBRUARY
S	M	T	W	T	F	S
				1	2	3	4
5	6	7	8	9	10	11
12	13	14	15	16	17	18
19	20	21	22	23	24	25
26	27	28				

MARCH
S	M	T	W	T	F	S
			1	2	3	4
5	6	7	8	9	10	11
12	13	14	15	16	17	18
19	20	21	22	23	24	25
26	27	28	29	30	31	

APRIL
S	M	T	W	T	F	S
						1
2	3	4	5	6	7	8
9	10	11	12	13	14	15
16	17	18	19	20	21	22
23	24	25	26	27	28	29
30						

MAY
S	M	T	W	T	F	S
	1	2	3	4	5	6
7	8	9	10	11	12	13
14	15	16	17	18	19	20
21	22	23	24	25	26	27
28	29	30	31			

JUNE
S	M	T	W	T	F	S
					1	2	3
4	5	6	7	8	9	10
11	12	13	14	15	16	17
18	19	20	21	22	23	24
25	26	27	28	29	30	

1911 1922 1933 1939 1950 1961 1967 A
1978 1989 1995 2006 2017 2023 2034
2045

JULY
S	M	T	W	T	F	S
						1
2	3	4	5	6	7	8
9	10	11	12	13	14	15
16	17	18	19	20	21	22
23	24	25	26	27	28	29
30	31					

AUGUST
S	M	T	W	T	F	S
		1	2	3	4	5
6	7	8	9	10	11	12
13	14	15	16	17	18	19
20	21	22	23	24	25	26
27	28	29	30	31		

SEPTEMBER
S	M	T	W	T	F	S
					1	2
3	4	5	6	7	8	9
10	11	12	13	14	15	16
17	18	19	20	21	22	23
24	25	26	27	28	29	30

OCTOBER
S	M	T	W	T	F	S
1	2	3	4	5	6	7
8	9	10	11	12	13	14
15	16	17	18	19	20	21
22	23	24	25	26	27	28
29	30	31				

NOVEMBER
S	M	T	W	T	F	S
			1	2	3	4
5	6	7	8	9	10	11
12	13	14	15	16	17	18
19	20	21	22	23	24	25
26	27	28	29	30		

DECEMBER
S	M	T	W	T	F	S
					1	2
3	4	5	6	7	8	9
10	11	12	13	14	15	16
17	18	19	20	21	22	23
24	25	26	27	28	29	30
31						

B 1781 1787 1798 1810 1821 1827 1838
       1849 1855 1866 1877 1883 1894 1900

JANUARY

S	M	T	W	T	F	S
		1	2	3	4	5	6
7	8	9	10	11	12	13
14	15	16	17	18	19	20
21	22	23	24	25	26	27
28	29	30	31			

FEBRUARY

S	M	T	W	T	F	S
					1	2	3
4	5	6	7	8	9	10
11	12	13	14	15	16	17
18	19	20	21	22	23	24
25	26	27	28			

MARCH

S	M	T	W	T	F	S
				1	2	3
4	5	6	7	8	9	10
11	12	13	14	15	16	17
18	19	20	21	22	23	24
25	26	27	28	29	30	31

APRIL

S	M	T	W	T	F	S
1	2	3	4	5	6	7
8	9	10	11	12	13	14
15	16	17	18	19	20	21
22	23	24	25	26	27	28
29	30					

MAY

S	M	T	W	T	F	S
		1	2	3	4	5
6	7	8	9	10	11	12
13	14	15	16	17	18	19
20	21	22	23	24	25	26
27	28	29	30	31		

JUNE

S	M	T	W	T	F	S
					1	2
3	4	5	6	7	8	9
10	11	12	13	14	15	16
17	18	19	20	21	22	23
24	25	26	27	28	29	30

**1906 1917 1923 1934 1945 1951 1962
1973 1979 1990 2001 2007 2018 2029
2035 2046** **B**

JULY
S	M	T	W	T	F	S
	1	2	3	4	5	6	7
1	2	3	4	5	6	7
8	9	10	11	12	13	14
15	16	17	18	19	20	21
22	23	24	25	26	27	28
29	30	31

AUGUST
S	M	T	W	T	F	S
				1	2	3	4
5	6	7	8	9	10	11
12	13	14	15	16	17	18
19	20	21	22	23	24	25
26	27	28	29	30	31

SEPTEMBER
S	M	T	W	T	F	S
						1
2	3	4	5	6	7	8
9	10	11	12	13	14	15
16	17	18	19	20	21	22
23	24	25	26	27	28	29
30

OCTOBER
S	M	T	W	T	F	S
	1	2	3	4	5	6
7	8	9	10	11	12	13
14	15	16	17	18	19	20
21	22	23	24	25	26	27
28	29	30	31

NOVEMBER
S	M	T	W	T	F	S
				1	2	3
4	5	6	7	8	9	10
11	12	13	14	15	16	17
18	19	20	21	22	23	24
25	26	27	28	29	30

DECEMBER
S	M	T	W	T	F	S
						1
2	3	4	5	6	7	8
9	10	11	12	13	14	15
16	17	18	19	20	21	22
23	24	25	26	27	28	29
30	31

C 1782 1793 1799 1805 1811 1822 1833
1839 1850 1861 1867 1878 1889 1895

JANUARY
S	M	T	W	T	F	S
		1	2	3	4	5
6	7	8	9	10	11	12
13	14	15	16	17	18	19
20	21	22	23	24	25	26
27	28	29	30	31		

FEBRUARY
S	M	T	W	T	F	S
					1	2
3	4	5	6	7	8	9
10	11	12	13	14	15	16
17	18	19	20	21	22	23
24	25	26	27	28		

MARCH
S	M	T	W	T	F	S
					1	2
3	4	5	6	7	8	9
10	11	12	13	14	15	16
17	18	19	20	21	22	23
24	25	26	27	28	29	30
31						

APRIL
S	M	T	W	T	F	S
	1	2	3	4	5	6
7	8	9	10	11	12	13
14	15	16	17	18	19	20
21	22	23	24	25	26	27
28	29	30				

MAY
S	M	T	W	T	F	S
			1	2	3	4
5	6	7	8	9	10	11
12	13	14	15	16	17	18
19	20	21	22	23	24	25
26	27	28	29	30	31	

JUNE
S	M	T	W	T	F	S
						1
2	3	4	5	6	7	8
9	10	11	12	13	14	15
16	17	18	19	20	21	22
23	24	25	26	27	28	29
30						

**1901 1907 1918 1929 1935 1946 1957
1963 1974 1985 1991 2002 2013 2019 C
2030 2041**

JULY
S	M	T	W	T	F	S
	1	2	3	4	5	6
7	8	9	10	11	12	13
14	15	16	17	18	19	20
21	22	23	24	25	26	27
28	29	30	31			

AUGUST
S	M	T	W	T	F	S
				1	2	3
4	5	6	7	8	9	10
11	12	13	14	15	16	17
18	19	20	21	22	23	24
25	26	27	28	29	30	31

SEPTEMBER
S	M	T	W	T	F	S
1	2	3	4	5	6	7
8	9	10	11	12	13	14
15	16	17	18	19	20	21
22	23	24	25	26	27	28
29	30					

OCTOBER
S	M	T	W	T	F	S
		1	2	3	4	5
6	7	8	9	10	11	12
13	14	15	16	17	18	19
20	21	22	23	24	25	26
27	28	29	30	31		

NOVEMBER
S	M	T	W	T	F	S
					1	2
3	4	5	6	7	8	9
10	11	12	13	14	15	16
17	18	19	20	21	22	23
24	25	26	27	28	29	30

DECEMBER
S	M	T	W	T	F	S
1	2	3	4	5	6	7
8	9	10	11	12	13	14
15	16	17	18	19	20	21
22	23	24	25	26	27	28
29	30	31				

162

D 1783 1794 1800 1806 1817 1823 1834
   1845 1851 1862 1873 1879 1890 1902

JANUARY

S	M	T	W	T	F	S
			1	2	3	4
5	6	7	8	9	10	11
12	13	14	15	16	17	18
19	20	21	22	23	24	25
26	27	28	29	30	31	

FEBRUARY

S	M	T	W	T	F	S
						1
2	3	4	5	6	7	8
9	10	11	12	13	14	15
16	17	18	19	20	21	22
23	24	25	26	27	28	

MARCH

S	M	T	W	T	F	S
						1
2	3	4	5	6	7	8
9	10	11	12	13	14	15
16	17	18	19	20	21	22
23	24	25	26	27	28	29
30	31					

APRIL

S	M	T	W	T	F	S
		1	2	3	4	5
6	7	8	9	10	11	12
13	14	15	16	17	18	19
20	21	22	23	24	25	26
27	28	29	30			

MAY

S	M	T	W	T	F	S
				1	2	3
4	5	6	7	8	9	10
11	12	13	14	15	16	17
18	19	20	21	22	23	24
25	26	27	28	29	30	31

JUNE

S	M	T	W	T	F	S
1	2	3	4	5	6	7
8	9	10	11	12	13	14
15	16	17	18	19	20	21
22	23	24	25	26	27	28
29	30					

1913 1919 1930 1941 1947 1958 1969
1975 1986 1997 2003 2014 2025 2031 **D**
2042

JULY
S	M	T	W	T	F	S
		1	2	3	4	5
6	7	8	9	10	11	12
13	14	15	16	17	18	19
20	21	22	23	24	25	26
27	28	29	30	31		

AUGUST
S	M	T	W	T	F	S
					1	2
3	4	5	6	7	8	9
10	11	12	13	14	15	16
17	18	19	20	21	22	23
24	25	26	27	28	29	30
31						

SEPTEMBER
S	M	T	W	T	F	S
	1	2	3	4	5	6
7	8	9	10	11	12	13
14	15	16	17	18	19	20
21	22	23	24	25	26	27
28	29	30				

OCTOBER
S	M	T	W	T	F	S
			1	2	3	4
5	6	7	8	9	10	11
12	13	14	15	16	17	18
19	20	21	22	23	24	25
26	27	28	29	30	31	

NOVEMBER
S	M	T	W	T	F	S
						1
2	3	4	5	6	7	8
9	10	11	12	13	14	15
16	17	18	19	20	21	22
23	24	25	26	27	28	29
30						

DECEMBER
S	M	T	W	T	F	S
	1	2	3	4	5	6
7	8	9	10	11	12	13
14	15	16	17	18	19	20
21	22	23	24	25	26	27
28	29	30	31			

E 1789 1795 1801 1807 1818 1829 1835
     1846 1857 1863 1874 1885 1891 1903

JANUARY
S	M	T	W	T	F	S
				1	2	3
4	5	6	7	8	9	10
11	12	13	14	15	16	17
18	19	20	21	22	23	24
25	26	27	28	29	30	31

FEBRUARY
S	M	T	W	T	F	S
1	2	3	4	5	6	7
8	9	10	11	12	13	14
15	16	17	18	19	20	21
22	23	24	25	26	27	28

MARCH
S	M	T	W	T	F	S
1	2	3	4	5	6	7
8	9	10	11	12	13	14
15	16	17	18	19	20	21
22	23	24	25	26	27	28
29	30	31				

APRIL
S	M	T	W	T	F	S
			1	2	3	4
5	6	7	8	9	10	11
12	13	14	15	16	17	18
19	20	21	22	23	24	25
26	27	28	29	30		

MAY
S	M	T	W	T	F	S
					1	2
3	4	5	6	7	8	9
10	11	12	13	14	15	16
17	18	19	20	21	22	23
24	25	26	27	28	29	30
31						

JUNE
S	M	T	W	T	F	S
	1	2	3	4	5	6
7	8	9	10	11	12	13
14	15	16	17	18	19	20
21	22	23	24	25	26	27
28	29	30				

**1914 1925 1931 1942 1953 1959 1970
1981 1987 1998 2009 2015 2026 2037
2043** **E**

JULY

S	M	T	W	T	F	S
			1	2	3	4
5	6	7	8	9	10	11
12	13	14	15	16	17	18
19	20	21	22	23	24	25
26	27	28	29	30	31	

AUGUST

S	M	T	W	T	F	S
						1
2	3	4	5	6	7	8
9	10	11	12	13	14	15
16	17	18	19	20	21	22
23	24	25	26	27	28	29
30	31					

SEPTEMBER

S	M	T	W	T	F	S
		1	2	3	4	5
6	7	8	9	10	11	12
13	14	15	16	17	18	19
20	21	22	23	24	25	26
27	28	29	30			

OCTOBER

S	M	T	W	T	F	S
					1	2
3	4	5	6	7	8	9
10	11	12	13	14	15	16
17	18	19	20	21	22	23
24	25	26	27	28	29	30
31						

NOVEMBER

S	M	T	W	T	F	S
1	2	3	4	5	6	7
8	9	10	11	12	13	14
15	16	17	18	19	20	21
22	23	24	25	26	27	28
29	30					

DECEMBER

S	M	T	W	T	F	S
		1	2	3	4	5
6	7	8	9	10	11	12
13	14	15	16	17	18	19
20	21	22	23	24	25	26
27	28	29	30	31		

F   1790 1802 1813 1819 1830 1841 1847
       1858 1869 1875 1886 1897 1909 1915

JANUARY

S	M	T	W	T	F	S
					1	2
3	4	5	6	7	8	9
10	11	12	13	14	15	16
17	18	19	20	21	22	23
24	25	26	27	28	29	30
31						

FEBRUARY

S	M	T	W	T	F	S
	1	2	3	4	5	6
7	8	9	10	11	12	13
14	15	16	17	18	19	20
21	22	23	24	25	26	27
28						

MARCH

S	M	T	W	T	F	S
	1	2	3	4	5	6
7	8	9	10	11	12	13
14	15	16	17	18	19	20
21	22	23	24	25	26	27
28	29	30	31			

APRIL

S	M	T	W	T	F	S
				1	2	3
4	5	6	7	8	9	10
11	12	13	14	15	16	17
18	19	20	21	22	23	24
25	26	27	28	29	30	

MAY

S	M	T	W	T	F	S
						1
2	3	4	5	6	7	8
9	10	11	12	13	14	15
16	17	18	19	20	21	22
23	24	25	26	27	28	29
30	31					

JUNE

S	M	T	W	T	F	S
		1	2	3	4	5
6	7	8	9	10	11	12
13	14	15	16	17	18	19
20	21	22	23	24	25	26
27	28	29	30			

1926 1937 1943 1954 1965 1971 1982
1993 1999 2010 2021 2027 2038 **F**

JULY
S	M	T	W	T	F	S
				1	2	3
4	5	6	7	8	9	10
11	12	13	14	15	16	17
18	19	20	21	22	23	24
25	26	27	28	29	30	31

AUGUST
S	M	T	W	T	F	S
1	2	3	4	5	6	7
8	9	10	11	12	13	14
15	16	17	18	19	20	21
22	23	24	25	26	27	28
29	30	31				

SEPTEMBER
S	M	T	W	T	F	S
			1	2	3	4
5	6	7	8	9	10	11
12	13	14	15	16	17	18
19	20	21	22	23	24	25
26	27	28	29	30		

OCTOBER
S	M	T	W	T	F	S
					1	2
3	4	5	6	7	8	9
10	11	12	13	14	15	16
17	18	19	20	21	22	23
24	25	26	27	28	29	30
31						

NOVEMBER
S	M	T	W	T	F	S
	1	2	3	4	5	6
7	8	9	10	11	12	13
14	15	16	17	18	19	20
21	22	23	24	25	26	27
28	29	30				

DECEMBER
S	M	T	W	T	F	S
				1	2	3	4
5	6	7	8	9	10	11
12	13	14	15	16	17	18
19	20	21	22	23	24	25
26	27	28	29	30	31	

G 1785 1791 1803 1814 1825 1831 1842
1853 1859 1870 1881 1887 1898 1910

JANUARY

S	M	T	W	T	F	S
						1
2	3	4	5	6	7	8
9	10	11	12	13	14	15
16	17	18	19	20	21	22
23	24	25	26	27	28	29
30	31					

FEBRUARY

S	M	T	W	T	F	S
		1	2	3	4	5
6	7	8	9	10	11	12
13	14	15	16	17	18	19
20	21	22	23	24	25	26
27	28					

MARCH

S	M	T	W	T	F	S
		1	2	3	4	5
6	7	8	9	10	11	12
13	14	15	16	17	18	19
20	21	22	23	24	25	26
27	28	29	30	31		

APRIL

S	M	T	W	T	F	S
					1	2
3	4	5	6	7	8	9
10	11	12	13	14	15	16
17	18	19	20	21	22	23
24	25	26	27	28	29	30

MAY

S	M	T	W	T	F	S
1	2	3	4	5	6	7
8	9	10	11	12	13	14
15	16	17	18	19	20	21
22	23	24	25	26	27	28
29	30	31				

JUNE

S	M	T	W	T	F	S
			1	2	3	4
5	6	7	8	9	10	11
12	13	14	15	16	17	18
19	20	21	22	23	24	25
26	27	28	29	30		

1921 1927 1938 1949 1955 1966 1977
1983 1994 2005 2011 2022 2033 2039 **G**

JULY

S	M	T	W	T	F	S
					1	2
3	4	5	6	7	8	9
10	11	12	13	14	15	16
17	18	19	20	21	22	23
24	25	26	27	28	29	30
31						

AUGUST

S	M	T	W	T	F	S
	1	2	3	4	5	6
7	8	9	10	11	12	13
14	15	16	17	18	19	20
21	22	23	24	25	26	27
28	29	30	31			

SEPTEMBER

S	M	T	W	T	F	S
				1	2	3
4	5	6	7	8	9	10
11	12	13	14	15	16	17
18	19	20	21	22	23	24
25	26	27	28	29	30	

OCTOBER

S	M	T	W	T	F	S
						1
2	3	4	5	6	7	8
9	10	11	12	13	14	15
16	17	18	19	20	21	22
23	24	25	26	27	28	29
30	31					

NOVEMBER

S	M	T	W	T	F	S
		1	2	3	4	5
6	7	8	9	10	11	12
13	14	15	16	17	18	19
20	21	22	23	24	25	26
27	28	29	30			

DECEMBER

S	M	T	W	T	F	S
				1	2	3
4	5	6	7	8	9	10
11	12	13	14	15	16	17
18	19	20	21	22	23	24
25	26	27	28	29	30	31

H 1792 1804 1832 1860 1888
       1928 1956 1984 2012 2040

JANUARY
S	M	T	W	T	F	S
	1	2	3	4	5	6	7
1	2	3	4	5	6	7
8	9	10	11	12	13	14
15	16	17	18	19	20	21
22	23	24	25	26	27	28
29	30	31				

FEBRUARY
S	M	T	W	T	F	S
			1	2	3	4
5	6	7	8	9	10	11
12	13	14	15	16	17	18
19	20	21	22	23	24	25
26	27	28	29			

MARCH
S	M	T	W	T	F	S
				1	2	3
4	5	6	7	8	9	10
11	12	13	14	15	16	17
18	19	20	21	22	23	24
25	26	27	28	29	30	31

APRIL
S	M	T	W	T	F	S
1	2	3	4	5	6	7
8	9	10	11	12	13	14
15	16	17	18	19	20	21
22	23	24	25	26	27	28
29	30					

MAY
S	M	T	W	T	F	S
		1	2	3	4	5
6	7	8	9	10	11	12
13	14	15	16	17	18	19
20	21	22	23	24	25	26
27	28	29	30	31		

JUNE
S	M	T	W	T	F	S
					1	2
3	4	5	6	7	8	9
10	11	12	13	14	15	16
17	18	19	20	21	22	23
24	25	26	27	28	29	30

H

JULY
S	M	T	W	T	F	S
1	2	3	4	5	6	7
8	9	10	11	12	13	14
15	16	17	18	19	20	21
22	23	24	25	26	27	28
29	30	31				

AUGUST
S	M	T	W	T	F	S
				1	2	3	4
5	6	7	8	9	10	11
12	13	14	15	16	17	18
19	20	21	22	23	24	25
26	27	28	29	30	31	

SEPTEMBER
S	M	T	W	T	F	S
						1
2	3	4	5	6	7	8
9	10	11	12	13	14	15
16	17	18	19	20	21	22
23	24	25	26	27	28	29
30						

OCTOBER
S	M	T	W	T	F	S
	1	2	3	4	5	6
7	8	9	10	11	12	13
14	15	16	17	18	19	20
21	22	23	24	25	26	27
28	29	30	31			

NOVEMBER
S	M	T	W	T	F	S
				1	2	3
4	5	6	7	8	9	10
11	12	13	14	15	16	17
18	19	20	21	22	23	24
25	26	27	28	29	30	

DECEMBER
S	M	T	W	T	F	S
						1
2	3	4	5	6	7	8
9	10	11	12	13	14	15
16	17	18	19	20	21	22
23	24	25	26	27	28	29
30	31					

I 1816 1844 1872 1912
       1940 1968 1996 2024

JANUARY
S	M	T	W	T	F	S
	1	2	3	4	5	6
7	8	9	10	11	12	13
14	15	16	17	18	19	20
21	22	23	24	25	26	27
28	29	30	31			

FEBRUARY
S	M	T	W	T	F	S
				1	2	3
4	5	6	7	8	9	10
11	12	13	14	15	16	17
18	19	20	21	22	23	24
25	26	27	28	29		

MARCH
S	M	T	W	T	F	S
					1	2
3	4	5	6	7	8	9
10	11	12	13	14	15	16
17	18	19	20	21	22	23
24	25	26	27	28	29	30
31						

APRIL
S	M	T	W	T	F	S
	1	2	3	4	5	6
7	8	9	10	11	12	13
14	15	16	17	18	19	20
21	22	23	24	25	26	27
28	29	30				

MAY
S	M	T	W	T	F	S
			1	2	3	4
5	6	7	8	9	10	11
12	13	14	15	16	17	18
19	20	21	22	23	24	25
26	27	28	29	30	31	

JUNE
S	M	T	W	T	F	S
						1
2	3	4	5	6	7	8
9	10	11	12	13	14	15
16	17	18	19	20	21	22
23	24	25	26	27	28	29
30						

I

JULY

S	M	T	W	T	F	S
		1	2	3	4	5	6
7	8	9	10	11	12	13
14	15	16	17	18	19	20
21	22	23	24	25	26	27
28	29	30	31			

AUGUST

S	M	T	W	T	F	S
					1	2	3
4	5	6	7	8	9	10
11	12	13	14	15	16	17
18	19	20	21	22	23	24
25	26	27	28	29	30	31

SEPTEMBER

S	M	T	W	T	F	S
1	2	3	4	5	6	7
8	9	10	11	12	13	14
15	16	17	18	19	20	21
22	23	24	25	26	27	28
29	30					

OCTOBER

S	M	T	W	T	F	S
		1	2	3	4	5
6	7	8	9	10	11	12
13	14	15	16	17	18	19
20	21	22	23	24	25	26
27	28	29	30	31		

NOVEMBER

S	M	T	W	T	F	S
					1	2
3	4	5	6	7	8	9
10	11	12	13	14	15	16
17	18	19	20	21	22	23
24	25	26	27	28	29	30

DECEMBER

S	M	T	W	T	F	S
1	2	3	4	5	6	7
8	9	10	11	12	13	14
15	16	17	18	19	20	21
22	23	24	25	26	27	28
29	30	31				

J 1788 1828 1856 1884 1924
      1952 1980 2008 2036

JANUARY
S	M	T	W	T	F	S
		1	2	3	4	5
6	7	8	9	10	11	12
13	14	15	16	17	18	19
20	21	22	23	24	25	26
27	28	29	30	31		

FEBRUARY
S	M	T	W	T	F	S
					1	2
3	4	5	6	7	8	9
10	11	12	13	14	15	16
17	18	19	20	21	22	23
24	25	26	27	28	29	

MARCH
S	M	T	W	T	F	S
						1
2	3	4	5	6	7	8
9	10	11	12	13	14	15
16	17	18	19	20	21	22
23	24	25	26	27	28	29
30	31					

APRIL
S	M	T	W	T	F	S
		1	2	3	4	5
6	7	8	9	10	11	12
13	14	15	16	17	18	19
20	21	22	23	24	25	26
27	28	29	30			

MAY
S	M	T	W	T	F	S
				1	2	3
4	5	6	7	8	9	10
11	12	13	14	15	16	17
18	19	20	21	22	23	24
25	26	27	28	29	30	31

JUNE
S	M	T	W	T	F	S
1	2	3	4	5	6	7
8	9	10	11	12	13	14
15	16	17	18	19	20	21
22	23	24	25	26	27	28
29	30					

J

JULY
S	M	T	W	T	F	S
		1	2	3	4	5
6	7	8	9	10	11	12
13	14	15	16	17	18	19
20	21	22	23	24	25	26
27	28	29	30	31		

AUGUST
S	M	T	W	T	F	S
					1	2
3	4	5	6	7	8	9
10	11	12	13	14	15	16
17	18	19	20	21	22	23
24	25	26	27	28	29	30
31						

SEPTEMBER
S	M	T	W	T	F	S
	1	2	3	4	5	6
7	8	9	10	11	12	13
14	15	16	17	18	19	20
21	22	23	24	25	26	27
28	29	30				

OCTOBER
S	M	T	W	T	F	S
			1	2	3	4
5	6	7	8	9	10	11
12	13	14	15	16	17	18
19	20	21	22	23	24	25
26	27	28	29	30	31	

NOVEMBER
S	M	T	W	T	F	S
						1
2	3	4	5	6	7	8
9	10	11	12	13	14	15
16	17	18	19	20	21	22
23	24	25	26	27	28	29
30						

DECEMBER
S	M	T	W	T	F	S
	1	2	3	4	5	6
7	8	9	10	11	12	13
14	15	16	17	18	19	20
21	22	23	24	25	26	27
28	29	30	31			

K 1812 1840 1868 1896 1908
1936 1964 1992 2020

JANUARY
S	M	T	W	T	F	S
			1	2	3	4
5	6	7	8	9	10	11
12	13	14	15	16	17	18
19	20	21	22	23	24	25
26	27	28	29	30	31	

FEBRUARY
S	M	T	W	T	F	S
						1
2	3	4	5	6	7	8
9	10	11	12	13	14	15
16	17	18	19	20	21	22
23	24	25	26	27	28	29

MARCH
S	M	T	W	T	F	S
1	2	3	4	5	6	7
8	9	10	11	12	13	14
15	16	17	18	19	20	21
22	23	24	25	26	27	28
29	30	31				

APRIL
S	M	T	W	T	F	S
			1	2	3	4
5	6	7	8	9	10	11
12	13	14	15	16	17	18
19	20	21	22	23	24	25
26	27	28	29	30		

MAY
S	M	T	W	T	F	S
					1	2
3	4	5	6	7	8	9
10	11	12	13	14	15	16
17	18	19	20	21	22	23
24	25	26	27	28	29	30
31						

JUNE
S	M	T	W	T	F	S
	1	2	3	4	5	6
7	8	9	10	11	12	13
14	15	16	17	18	19	20
21	22	23	24	25	26	27
28	29	30				

K

JULY

S	M	T	W	T	F	S
			1	2	3	4
5	6	7	8	9	10	11
12	13	14	15	16	17	18
19	20	21	22	23	24	25
26	27	28	29	30	31	

AUGUST

S	M	T	W	T	F	S
						1
2	3	4	5	6	7	8
9	10	11	12	13	14	15
16	17	18	19	20	21	22
23	24	25	26	27	28	29
30	31					

SEPTEMBER

S	M	T	W	T	F	S
		1	2	3	4	5
6	7	8	9	10	11	12
13	14	15	16	17	18	19
20	21	22	23	24	25	26
27	28	29	30			

OCTOBER

S	M	T	W	T	F	S
				1	2	3
4	5	6	7	8	9	10
11	12	13	14	15	16	17
18	19	20	21	22	23	24
25	26	27	28	29	30	31

NOVEMBER

S	M	T	W	T	F	S
1	2	3	4	5	6	7
8	9	10	11	12	13	14
15	16	17	18	19	20	21
22	23	24	25	26	27	28
29	30					

DECEMBER

S	M	T	W	T	F	S
		1	2	3	4	5
6	7	8	9	10	11	12
13	14	15	16	17	18	19
20	21	22	23	24	25	26
27	28	29	30	31		

L 1784 1824 1852 1880 1920
       1948 1976 2004 2032

JANUARY
S	M	T	W	T	F	S
				1	2	3
4	5	6	7	8	9	10
11	12	13	14	15	16	17
18	19	20	21	22	23	24
25	26	27	28	29	30	31

FEBRUARY
S	M	T	W	T	F	S
1	2	3	4	5	6	7
8	9	10	11	12	13	14
15	16	17	18	19	20	21
22	23	24	25	26	27	28
29						

MARCH
S	M	T	W	T	F	S
	1	2	3	4	5	6
7	8	9	10	11	12	13
14	15	16	17	18	19	20
21	22	23	24	25	26	27
28	29	30	31			

APRIL
S	M	T	W	T	F	S
				1	2	3
4	5	6	7	8	9	10
11	12	13	14	15	16	17
18	19	20	21	22	23	24
25	26	27	28	29	30	

MAY
S	M	T	W	T	F	S
						1
2	3	4	5	6	7	8
9	10	11	12	13	14	15
16	17	18	19	20	21	22
23	24	25	26	27	28	29
30	31					

JUNE
S	M	T	W	T	F	S
		1	2	3	4	5
6	7	8	9	10	11	12
13	14	15	16	17	18	19
20	21	22	23	24	25	26
27	28	29	30			

L

JULY

S	M	T	W	T	F	S
				1	2	3
4	5	6	7	8	9	10
11	12	13	14	15	16	17
18	19	20	21	22	23	24
25	26	27	28	29	30	31

AUGUST

S	M	T	W	T	F	S
1	2	3	4	5	6	7
8	9	10	11	12	13	14
15	16	17	18	19	20	21
22	23	24	25	26	27	28
29	30	31				

SEPTEMBER

S	M	T	W	T	F	S
			1	2	3	4
5	6	7	8	9	10	11
12	13	14	15	16	17	18
19	20	21	22	23	24	25
26	27	28	29	30		

OCTOBER

S	M	T	W	T	F	S
					1	2
3	4	5	6	7	8	9
10	11	12	13	14	15	16
17	18	19	20	21	22	23
24	25	26	27	28	29	30
31						

NOVEMBER

S	M	T	W	T	F	S
	1	2	3	4	5	6
7	8	9	10	11	12	13
14	15	16	17	18	19	20
21	22	23	24	25	26	27
28	29	30				

DECEMBER

S	M	T	W	T	F	S
			1	2	3	4
5	6	7	8	9	10	11
12	13	14	15	16	17	18
19	20	21	22	23	24	25
26	27	28	29	30	31	

M 1796 1808 1836 1864 1892 1904
1932 1960 1988 2016 2044

JANUARY

S	M	T	W	T	F	S
					1	2
3	4	5	6	7	8	9
10	11	12	13	14	15	16
17	18	19	20	21	22	23
24	25	26	27	28	29	30
31						

FEBRUARY

S	M	T	W	T	F	S
	1	2	3	4	5	6
7	8	9	10	11	12	13
14	15	16	17	18	19	20
21	22	23	24	25	26	27
28	29					

MARCH

S	M	T	W	T	F	S
		1	2	3	4	5
6	7	8	9	10	11	12
13	14	15	16	17	18	19
20	21	22	23	24	25	26
27	28	29	30	31		

APRIL

S	M	T	W	T	F	S
					1	2
3	4	5	6	7	8	9
10	11	12	13	14	15	16
17	18	19	20	21	22	23
24	25	26	27	28	29	30

MAY

S	M	T	W	T	F	S
1	2	3	4	5	6	7
8	9	10	11	12	13	14
15	16	17	18	19	20	21
22	23	24	25	26	27	28
29	30	31				

JUNE

S	M	T	W	T	F	S
			1	2	3	4
5	6	7	8	9	10	11
12	13	14	15	16	17	18
19	20	21	22	23	24	25
26	27	28	29	30		

M

JULY

S	M	T	W	T	F	S
					1	2
3	4	5	6	7	8	9
10	11	12	13	14	15	16
17	18	19	20	21	22	23
24	25	26	27	28	29	30
31						

AUGUST

S	M	T	W	T	F	S
	1	2	3	4	5	6
7	8	9	10	11	12	13
14	15	16	17	18	19	20
21	22	23	24	25	26	27
28	29	30	31			

SEPTEMBER

S	M	T	W	T	F	S
				1	2	3
4	5	6	7	8	9	10
11	12	13	14	15	16	17
18	19	20	21	22	23	24
25	26	27	28	29	30	

OCTOBER

S	M	T	W	T	F	S
						1
2	3	4	5	6	7	8
9	10	11	12	13	14	15
16	17	18	19	20	21	22
23	24	25	26	27	28	29
30	31					

NOVEMBER

S	M	T	W	T	F	S
		1	2	3	4	5
6	7	8	9	10	11	12
13	14	15	16	17	18	19
20	21	22	23	24	25	26
27	28	29	30			

DECEMBER

S	M	T	W	T	F	S
				1	2	3
4	5	6	7	8	9	10
11	12	13	14	15	16	17
18	19	20	21	22	23	24
25	26	27	28	29	30	31

N   1780 1820 1848 1876 1916
      1944 1972 2000 2028

JANUARY
S	M	T	W	T	F	S
						1
2	3	4	5	6	7	8
9	10	11	12	13	14	15
16	17	18	19	20	21	22
23	24	25	26	27	28	29
30	31					

FEBRUARY
S	M	T	W	T	F	S
			1	2	3	4	5
6	7	8	9	10	11	12
13	14	15	16	17	18	19
20	21	22	23	24	25	26
27	28	29				

MARCH
S	M	T	W	T	F	S
				1	2	3	4
5	6	7	8	9	10	11
12	13	14	15	16	17	18
19	20	21	22	23	24	25
26	27	28	29	30	31	

APRIL
S	M	T	W	T	F	S
						1
2	3	4	5	6	7	8
9	10	11	12	13	14	15
16	17	18	19	20	21	22
23	24	25	26	27	28	29
30						

MAY
S	M	T	W	T	F	S
	1	2	3	4	5	6
7	8	9	10	11	12	13
14	15	16	17	18	19	20
21	22	23	24	25	26	27
28	29	30	31			

JUNE
S	M	T	W	T	F	S
				1	2	3
4	5	6	7	8	9	10
11	12	13	14	15	16	17
18	19	20	21	22	23	24
25	26	27	28	29	30	

N

JULY

S	M	T	W	T	F	S
						1
2	3	4	5	6	7	8
9	10	11	12	13	14	15
16	17	18	19	20	21	22
23	24	25	26	27	28	29
30	31					

AUGUST

S	M	T	W	T	F	S
		1	2	3	4	5
6	7	8	9	10	11	12
13	14	15	16	17	18	19
20	21	22	23	24	25	26
27	28	29	30	31		

SEPTEMBER

S	M	T	W	T	F	S
					1	2
3	4	5	6	7	8	9
10	11	12	13	14	15	16
17	18	19	20	21	22	23
24	25	26	27	28	29	30

OCTOBER

S	M	T	W	T	F	S
1	2	3	4	5	6	7
8	9	10	11	12	13	14
15	16	17	18	19	20	21
22	23	24	25	26	27	28
29	30	31				

NOVEMBER

S	M	T	W	T	F	S
			1	2	3	4
5	6	7	8	9	10	11
12	13	14	15	16	17	18
19	20	21	22	23	24	25
26	27	28	29	30		

DECEMBER

S	M	T	W	T	F	S
					1	2
3	4	5	6	7	8	9
10	11	12	13	14	15	16
17	18	19	20	21	22	23
24	25	26	27	28	29	30
31						

Time zones of the world
Some countries, including the US, adopt Daylight
Saving Time (DST) in order to receive more daylight

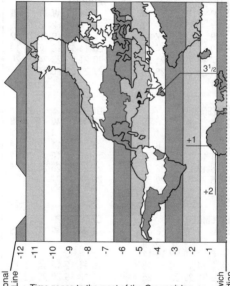

Time zones to the west of the Greenwich
Meridian are "earlier" than Greenwich Mean
Time (GMT). For example, at 12 noon GMT it
is 7 am in New York (A).

in summer. Clocks are put forward 1 hour in spring and back 1 hour in fall. The maps below do not reflect DST adjustments.

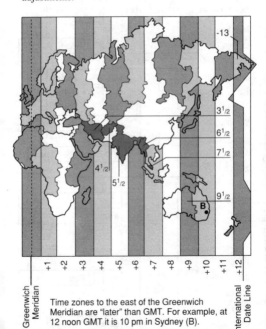

Time zones to the east of the Greenwich Meridian are "later" than GMT. For example, at 12 noon GMT it is 10 pm in Sydney (B).

Office times

The table shows the usual office hours (local time) in various cities around the world compared to New York

New York time	10	11	12	1AM	2	3	4	5	6	7
New York										
London							9:00am			
Sydney	◁ 9:00am		5:00pm							
Brussels						8:30am	12:00pm			
Rio de Janeiro										
Toronto										
Copenhagen					8:00am					
Paris						9:00am	12:00am			
Athens					8:00am				2:00pm	
Milan						8:30am	12:45pm			
Tokyo	◁ 9:00am			5:00pm						
Amsterdam						8:30am				
Oslo					8:00am					
Lisbon							10:00am	12:30pm		
Dublin							9:30am			
Riyadh					8:00am			1:00pm		
Johannesburg						8:30am				
Madrid							9:30am	1:30pm		
Stockholm					8:30am					
Geneva					8:00am	12:00pm				
Frankfurt					8:00am					

(east coast time). Los Angeles (west coast time) is
three hours behind.

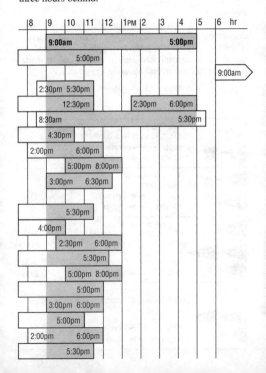

8: Speed

Formulas

Below are listed the multiplication/division factors for
converting units of speed from one measuring system
to another. Note that two kinds of factors are given:
quick, for an approximate conversion that can be made
without a calculator; and accurate, for an exact
conversion.

			Quick	**Accurate**
	Miles per hour (mph)			
	Kilometers per hour (km/h)			
	mph ⟶ km/h		× 1.5	× 1.609
	km/h ⟶ mph		÷ 1.5	× 0.621
	Yards per minute (ypm)			
	Meters per minute (m/min)			
	ypm ⟶ m/min		÷ 1	× 0.914
	m/min ⟶ ypm		× 1	× 1.094
	Feet per minute (ft/min)			
	Meters per minute (m/min)			
	ft/min ⟶ m/min		÷ 3	× 0.305
	m/min ⟶ ft/min		× 3	× 3.281
	Inches per second (in/s)			
	Centimeters per second (cm/s)			
	in/s ⟶ cm/s		× 2.5	× 2.54
	cm/s ⟶ in/s		÷ 2.5	× 0.394

	International knots (kn) Miles per hour (mph)	**Quick**	**Accurate**
kn $\longrightarrow$ mph		× 1	× 1.151
mph $\longrightarrow$ kn		÷ 1	× 0.869

	British knots (UK kn) International knots (kn)		
UK kn $\longrightarrow$ kn		× 1	× 1.001
kn $\longrightarrow$ UK kn		÷ 1	× 0.999

	International knots (kn) Kilometers per hour (km/h)		
kn $\longrightarrow$ km/h		× 2	× 1.852
km/h $\longrightarrow$ kn		÷ 2	× 0.540

	Miles per hour (mph) Feet per second (ft/s)		
mph $\longrightarrow$ ft/s		× 1.5	× 1.467
ft/s $\longrightarrow$ mph		÷ 1.5	× 0.682

	Kilometers per hour (km/h) Meters per second (m/s)		
km/h $\longrightarrow$ m/s		÷ 3.5	× 0.278
m/s $\longrightarrow$ km/h		× 3.5	× 3.599

Conversion tables

The tables below can be used to convert units of speed from one measuring system to another. The first group

Miles per hour to Kilometers per hour		Kilometers per hour to Miles per hour		Yards per minute to Meters per minute	
mph	km/h	km/h	mph	ypm	m/min
1	1.609	1	0.621	1	0.914
2	3.219	2	1.242	2	1.829
3	4.828	3	1.864	3	2.743
4	6.437	4	2.485	4	3.658
5	8.047	5	3.106	5	4.572
6	9.656	6	3.728	6	5.486
7	11.265	7	4.349	7	6.401
8	12.875	8	4.970	8	7.315
9	14.484	9	5.592	9	8.230
10	16.093	10	6.213	10	9.144
20	32.187	20	12.427	20	18.288
30	48.280	30	18.641	30	27.432
40	64.374	40	24.854	40	36.576
50	80.467	50	31.068	50	45.720
60	96.561	60	37.282	60	54.864
70	112.654	70	43.495	70	64.008
80	128.748	80	49.709	80	73.152
90	144.841	90	55.923	90	82.296
100	160.934	100	62.137	100	91.440

of tables converts US units/UK imperial units to metric, and vice versa. The tables beginning on page 192 convert knots, imperial, and metric units.

Meters per minute to Yards per minute		Feet per minute to Meters per minute		Meters per minute to Feet per minute	
m/min	ypm	ft/min	m/min	m/min	ft/min
1	1.094	1	0.305	1	3.281
2	2.187	2	0.610	2	6.562
3	3.281	3	0.914	3	9.842
4	4.374	4	1.219	4	13.123
5	5.468	5	1.524	5	16.404
6	6.562	6	1.829	6	19.685
7	7.655	7	2.134	7	22.966
8	8.749	8	2.438	8	26.246
9	9.842	9	2.743	9	29.527
10	10.936	10	3.048	10	32.808
20	21.872	20	6.096	20	65.616
30	32.808	30	9.144	30	98.424
40	43.744	40	12.192	40	131.232
50	54.680	50	15.240	50	164.040
60	65.616	60	18.288	60	196.848
70	76.552	70	21.336	70	229.656
80	87.488	80	24.384	80	262.464
90	98.424	90	27.432	90	295.272
100	109.360	100	30.480	100	328.080

US units/UK imperial and metric units of speed (continued)

Inches per second to Centimeters per second		Centimeters per second to Inches per second		International knots to Miles per hour	
in/s	cm/s	cm/s	in/s	kn	mph
1	2.54	1	0.394	1	1.151
2	5.08	2	0.787	2	2.302
3	7.62	3	1.181	3	3.452
4	10.16	4	1.579	4	4.603
5	12.70	5	1.969	5	5.753
6	15.24	6	2.362	6	6.905
7	17.78	7	2.760	7	8.055
8	20.32	8	3.150	8	9.206
9	22.86	9	3.543	9	10.357
10	25.40	10	3.937	10	11.508
20	50.80	20	7.874	20	23.016
30	76.20	30	11.811	30	34.523
40	101.60	40	15.748	40	46.031
50	127.00	50	19.685	50	57.540
60	152.40	60	23.622	60	69.047
70	177.80	70	27.559	70	80.555
80	203.20	80	31.496	80	92.062
90	228.60	90	35.433	90	103.570
100	254.00	100	39.370	100	115.078

Miles per hour to International knots		UK knots to International knots		International knots to UK knots	
mph	kn	UK kn	kn	kn	UK kn
1	0.869	1	1.001	1	0.999
2	1.738	2	2.001	2	1.999
3	2.607	3	3.002	3	2.998
4	3.476	4	4.003	4	3.997
5	4.345	5	5.003	5	4.997
6	5.214	6	6.004	6	5.996
7	6.083	7	7.004	7	6.996
8	6.952	8	8.005	8	7.995
9	7.821	9	9.006	9	8.994
10	8.690	10	10.006	10	9.994
20	17.380	20	20.013	20	19.987
30	26.069	30	30.019	30	29.981
40	34.759	40	40.026	40	39.974
50	43.449	50	50.032	50	49.968
60	52.139	60	60.038	60	59.962
70	60.828	70	70.045	70	69.955
80	69.518	80	80.051	80	79.949
90	78.208	90	90.058	90	89.942
100	86.898	100	100.064	100	99.936

**US units/UK imperial and metric units of speed
(continued)**

International knots to Kilometers per hour		Kilometers per hour to International knots		Miles per hour to Feet per second	
kn	km/h	km/h	kn	mph	ft/s
1	1.852	1	0.540	1	1.467
2	3.704	2	1.08	2	2.933
3	5.556	3	1.62	3	4.400
4	7.408	4	2.16	4	5.867
5	9.260	5	2.70	5	7.334
6	11.112	6	3.23	6	8.800
7	12.964	7	3.77	7	10.267
8	14.816	8	4.31	8	11.734
9	16.668	9	4.85	9	13.203
10	18.520	10	5.30	10	14.667
20	37.040	20	10.78	20	29.334
30	55.560	30	16.17	30	44.001
40	74.080	40	21.56	40	58.668
50	92.600	50	26.95	50	73.335
60	111.120	60	32.34	60	88.002
70	129.640	70	37.73	70	102.669
80	148.160	80	43.12	80	117.336
90	166.680	90	48.51	90	132.003
100	185.200	100	53.90	100	146.670

Feet per second to Miles per hour		Kilometers per hour to Meters per second		Meters per second to Kilometers per hour	
ft/s	mph	km/h	m/s	m/s	km/h
1	0.682	1	0.278	1	3.599
2	1.364	2	0.556	2	7.198
3	2.046	3	0.834	3	10.797
4	2.728	4	1.111	4	14.396
5	3.410	5	1.389	5	17.995
6	4.092	6	1.669	6	21.594
7	4.774	7	1.945	7	25.193
8	5.456	8	2.222	8	28.792
9	6.138	9	2.500	9	32.391
10	6.820	10	2.778	10	35.990
20	13.640	20	5.556	20	71.980
30	20.460	30	8.334	30	107.970
40	27.280	40	11.112	40	143.960
50	34.100	50	13.890	50	179.950
60	40.920	60	16.668	60	215.940
70	47.740	70	19.446	70	251.930
80	54.560	80	22.224	80	287.920
90	61.380	90	25.002	90	323.910
100	68.200	100	27.780	100	359.900

The Beaufort scale

The speed of wind is measured by using the Beaufort Scale, based on easily observable factors such as tree movement, smoke behavior, and damage incurred. It was devised by a 19th-century British admiral, Sir Francis Beaufort.

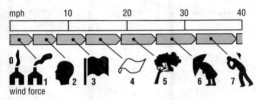

Number	Description	Speed range mph
Force 0	Calm	Below 1
Force 1	Light air	1–3
Force 2	Light breeze	4–7
Force 3	Gentle breeze	8–12
Force 4	Moderate breeze	13–18
Force 5	Fresh breeze	19–24
Force 6	Strong breeze	25–31
Force 7	Moderate gale	32–38
Force 8	Fresh gale	39–46
Force 9	Strong gale	47–54
Force 10	Whole gale	55–63
Force 11	Storm	64–75
Force 12	Hurricane	Over 75

As air moves across the surface of the Earth, its direction is determined by such factors as the Earth's rotation, variations in temperature, air pressure, and land features such as mountains. Listed below are examples showing the effects of wind as measured on the Beaufort Scale, the variety of winds that are measured, and the range of speeds to which they apply.

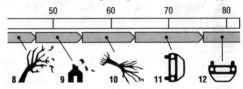

Number	Characteristics
Force 0	Smoke rises straight up
Force 1	Smoke shows wind direction
Force 2	Wind felt on face
Force 3	Flag extends
Force 4	Dust and paper blow in wind
Force 5	Small trees sway in wind
Force 6	Umbrellas are difficult to use
Force 7	Difficult to stand up in wind
Force 8	Twigs break off trees
Force 9	Chimney tops and tiles are dislodged
Force 10	Trees are uprooted
Force 11	Extensive damage
Force 12	Extremely violent

9: Geometry

Polygons

	Name of polygon	Number of sides	Each internal angle	Sum of internal angles
	Triangle	3	60°	180°
	Square	4	90°	360°
	Pentagon	5	108°	540°
	Hexagon	6	120°	720°
	Heptagon	7	128.6°	900°
	Octagon	8	135°	1,080°
	Nonagon	9	140°	1,260°
	Decagon	10	144°	1,440°
	Undecagon	11	147.3°	1,620°
	Dodecagon	12	150°	1,800°

A Triangle   **F** Octagon
B Square   **G** Nonagon
C Pentagon   **H** Decagon
D Hexagon   **I** Undecagon
E Heptagon   **J** Dodecagon

Quadrilaterals

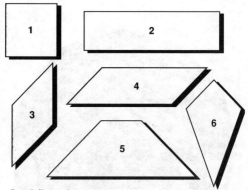

Quadrilaterals

A quadrilateral is a four-sided polygon.

1 Square	All the sides are the same length and all the angles are right angles.
2 Rectangle	Opposite sides are the same length and all the angles are right angles.
3 Rhombus	All the sides are the same length but none of the angles are right angles.
4 Parallelogram	Opposite sides are parallel to each other and of the same length.
5 Trapezoid	One pair of the opposite sides is parallel.
6 Kite	Adjacent sides are the same length and the diagonals intersect at right angles.

Triangles

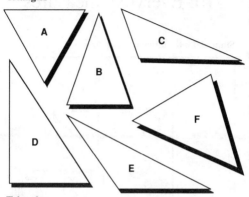

Triangles

A	Equilateral	All the sides are the same length and all the angles are equal.
B	Isosceles	Two sides are of the same length and two angles are of equal size.
C	Scalene	All the sides are of different length and all the angles are of different sizes.
D	Right angle	A triangle that contains one right angle.
E	Obtuse angle	A triangle that contains one obtuse angle.
F	Acute angle	A triangle with three acute angles.

10: Everyday measures

Standard international paper sizes

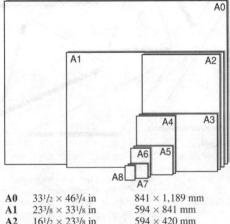

A0	$33^1/_2 \times 46^3/_4$ in	$841 \times 1,189$ mm
A1	$23^3/_8 \times 33^1/_8$ in	594×841 mm
A2	$16^1/_2 \times 23^3/_8$ in	594×420 mm
A3	$11^3/_4 \times 16^1/_2$ in	297×420 mm
A4	$8^1/_4 \times 11^3/_4$ in	297×210 mm
A5	$5^7/_8 \times 8^1/_4$ in	148×210 mm
A6	$4^1/_8 \times 6$ in	148×105 mm
A7	$3 \times 4^1/_8$ in	74×105 mm
A8	2×3 in	74×52 mm

Stock paper sizes
Although special paper sizes may be ordered from
paper merchants, the grades of paper that are most
popular in the US are provided in standard sizes. These
standard sizes are measured in the metric system used
in Europe, as is the "A series" given on the previous
page.

Stock sizes for book paper
In the US, the sizes of the presses used for book
printing and the most popular book trim sizes dictate
the stock sizes for book paper. The figures for some of
these sizes are given below.

Sheet size	No. of pages per sheet	Folded size before trimming	Trim size
35×45 in	64	$5^5/_8 \times 8^3/_4$	$5^1/_2 \times 8^1/_2$
38×50 in	64	$6^1/_4 \times 9^1/_2$	$6^1/_8 \times 9^1/_4$
41×61 in	128	$5^1/_8 \times 7^5/_8$	$5 \times 7^3/_8$
44×66 in	128	$5^1/_2 \times 8^3/_4$	$5^3/_8 \times 8$
45×68 in	128	$5^5/_8 \times 8^1/_2$	$5^1/_2 \times 8^1/_4$
45×69 in	128	$5^3/_4 \times 8^5/_8$	$5^1/_8 \times 8^3/_8$

Envelope sizes and styles
There are two basic styles of envelope: open-end and open-side. Within these two categories, there are as many variations of style and size as there are uses. Here, a selection of styles is given, together with the smallest and largest sizes in which they are available.

Open-end envelopes

Catalog A strong envelope used for magazines, booklets, reports, and catalogs.
Smallest (glove): $3^7/8 \times 7^1/2$ in
Largest (catalog): $12 \times 15^1/2$ in

Clasp/string and button A strong, reusable catalog envelope, with a metal clasp or string and button, used for mailing bulky material.
Smallest: $2^1/2 \times 4^1/4$ in
Largest: $12 \times 15^1/2$ in

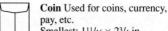

Coin Used for coins, currency, pay, etc.
Smallest: $1^{11}/16 \times 2^3/4$ in
Largest: $3^1/2 \times 6^1/2$ in

Open-side envelopes

Booklet Used for direct mailing, brochures, annual reports, sales literature, etc.
Smallest: $3^{1}/_4 \times 6^{3}/_4$ in
Largest: $9^{1}/_2 \times 12^{5}/_8$ in

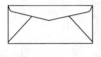

Commercial/official Used for all types of correspondence, both personal and official.
Smallest (commercial): $3^{1}/_{16} \times 5^{1}/_2$ in
Largest (official): $5 \times 11^{1}/_2$ in

Banker's flap Stronger than a commercial envelope.
Smallest: $3^{7}/_8 \times 7^{1}/_2$ in
Largest: 6×12 in

Baronial Used for invitations and greetings cards.
Smallest: $3^{5}/_8 \times 5^{1}/_8$ in
Largest (card): $4^{5}/_8 \times 6^{1}/_4$ in

Window envelopes

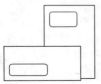

These are available in many different sizes and styles.

Book sizes

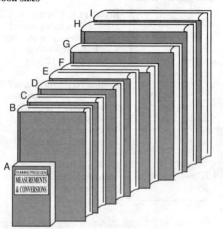

A	Running Press Gem	$3^1/_8 \times 4^5/_8$ in	117×79 mm

Octavo formats

B	$5^1/_4 \times 8^1/_2$ in	133×216 mm
C	$5^1/_2 \times 8^1/_2$ in	140×216 mm
D	6×9 in	152×229 mm
E	$6^1/_8 \times 9^1/_4$ in	156×235 mm

Quarto formats

F	7×9 in	178×229 mm
G	8×10 in	203×254 mm
H	$8^1/_4 \times 10^7/_8$ in	210×276 mm
I	$8^1/_2 \times 11$ in	216×279 mm

Wine bottle shapes

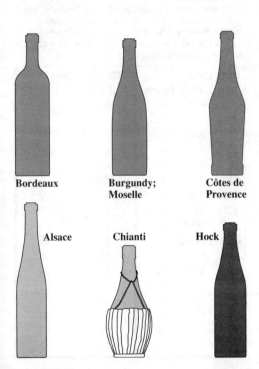

Bordeaux

Burgundy;
Moselle

Côtes de
Provence

Alsace

Chianti

Hock

Clothing sizes

US clothing sizes are equal to UK sizes for some items, such as children's shoes; for others, the two vary slightly. Below are listed the European equivalents of US and UK clothing and shoe sizes. Remember also that sizes vary depending on the manufacturer.

Men's shoes		
USA	UK	Europe
7	6 1/2	39
7 1/2	7	40
8	7 1/2	41
8 1/2	8	42
9	8 1/2	43
9 1/2	9	43
10	9 1/2	44
10 1/2	10	44
11	10 1/2	45

Women's shoes		
USA	UK	Europe
5	3 1/2	36
6	4 1/2	37
7	5 1/2	38
8	6 1/2	39
9	7 1/2	40

Children's shoes	
USA/UK	Europe
0	15
1	17
2	18
3	19
4	20
4 1/2	21
5	22
6	23
7	24
8	25
8 1/2	26
9	27
10	28
11	29
12	30
12 1/2	31
13	32

Men's suits/overcoats

USA/UK	Europe
36	46
38	48
40	50
42	52
44	54
46	56

Men's shirts

USA/UK	Europe
12	30–31
12$\frac{1}{2}$	32
13	33
13$\frac{1}{2}$	34–35
14	36
14$\frac{1}{2}$	37
15	38
15$\frac{1}{2}$	39–40
16	41
16$\frac{1}{2}$	42
17	43
17$\frac{1}{2}$	44–45

Men's socks

USA/UK	Europe
9	38–39
10	39–40
10$\frac{1}{2}$	40–41
11	41–42
11$\frac{1}{2}$	42–43

Women's clothing

USA	UK	Europe
6	8	36
8	10	38
10	12	40
12	14	42
14	16	44
16	18	46
18	20	48
20	22	50
22	24	52

Children's clothing

USA	UK	Europe
2	16–18	40–45
4	20–22	50–55
6	24–26	60–65
7	28–30	70–75
8	32–34	80–85
9	36–38	90–95

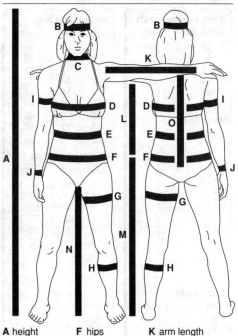

A height	**F** hips	**K** arm length
B head	**G** thigh	**L** armpit to hip
C neck	**H** calf	**M** outside leg
D chest/bust	**I** arm	**N** inside leg
E waist	**J** wrist	**O** back

Body measurements

The standard body measurements shown on the
diagram on the opposite page are those needed for
garment fitting.

Below are a few tips on taking some of these
measurements.

Neck

Measure at the fullest part.

Chest/bust

Measure at the fullest part of the bust or chest and
straight across the back.

Waist

Tie a string around the thinnest part of your body (the
waist) and leave it there as a point of reference for
other measurements.

Hips

There are two places to measure hips, depending on the
garment: one is 2–4 in below the waist, at the top of the
hipbones; the other is at the fullest part, usually
7–9 in below.

Arm

Measure at the fullest part, usually about 1 in below the
armpit.

Arm length

Start at the shoulder bone and continue past the elbow
to the wrist, with the arm slightly bent.

Back

Measure from the prominent bone in the back of the
neck down the center to the point at which you want
the garment to end, e.g. the hips.

Life expectancy

The table below shows life expectancy figures for
selected countries. Age in years appears at the top of
each bar.

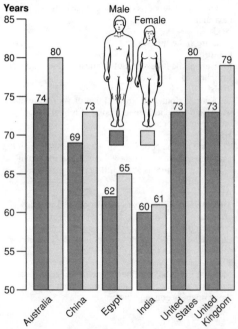

Average heights

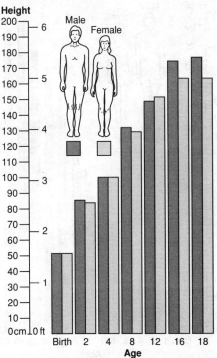

Average weights

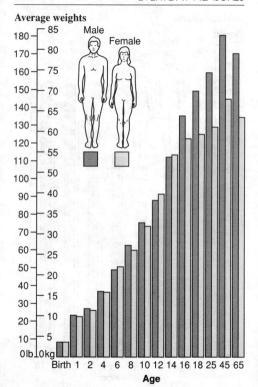

Laundry codes

Most garments contain a label giving laundering instructions (the International Textile Care Labeling Code [ITCL]), usually shown in terms of symbols, that tell you if any item is washable (or should be dry-cleaned) and how to wash it. The codes are listed below.

The table on the following pages lists the old and new codes, recommended temperatures (for machine- or hand-washing), and other machine settings, and the types of fabric that should be washed according to that code.

A Machine or hand wash	**F** Dry cleanable
B Can be bleached	**G** Do not dry clean
C Do not bleach	**H** Tumble dry
D Iron	**I** Do not tumble dry
E Do not iron	

OLD	NEW	MACHINE WASH	HAND WASH
CODE		TEMPERATURE	
1 **9** **95** **95**	95	Very hot 95 °C (203 °F) to boil	Hand hot 50 °C (122 °F) or boil
2 **3** **60** **60**	60	Hot 60 °C (140 °F)	Hand hot 50 °C (122 °F)
4 **50**	50	Hand hot 50 °C (122 °F)	Hand hot 50 °C (122 °F)
5 **40**	40	Warm 40 °C (104 °F)	Warm 40 °C (104 °F)
6 **40**	40	Warm 40 °C (104 °F)	Warm 40 °C (104 °F)
7 **40**	40	Warm 40 °C (104 °F)	Warm 40 °C (104 °F)
8 **30**	30 30	Cool 30 °C (86 °F)	Cool 30 °C (86 °F)

AGITATION	RINSE	SPIN	FABRIC
Maximum	Normal	Normal	White cotton and linen with no special finish
Maximum	Normal	Normal	Cotton, linen, viscose, color-fast with no special finish
Medium	Cold	Short spin or drip dry	Colored nylon, polyester, cotton, and viscose with special finish
Maximum	Normal	Normal	Cotton, linen, viscose, color-fast to 40 °C (104 °F)
Minimum	Cold	Short spin	Acrylics, acetate, and mixtures with wool
Minimum; do not rub	Normal	Normal; do not hand wring	Wool and wool mixtures
Minimum	Cold	Short spin; do not hand wring	Silk and printed acetate, not color-fast at 40 °C (104 °F)

Gun gauge/caliber

A shotgun bore (diameter) is expressed in terms of gauge. Gauge was originally determined by the number of round lead balls – each the size of the shotgun bore – in a pound. For example, a 10-gauge shotgun was one that used balls that were 10 to the pound. The exception is the 410 bore, which is measured in inches: .410 in diameter, using 67.5 gauge. The most popular size today is the 12-gauge.

The table below shows gauge and equivalent bore size.

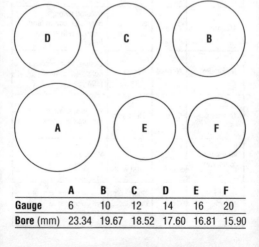

	A	B	C	D	E	F
Gauge	6	10	12	14	16	20
Bore (mm)	23.34	19.67	18.52	17.60	16.81	15.90

Horse measurements

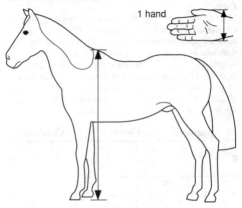

1 hand

The height of a horse or pony is measured to its withers (on the highest point on its back at the neck base), as shown above. Height is expressed in "hands high" (hh). One hand is 4 in (10 cm), the average width of a person's hand. Height is given to the nearest inch – a pony measuring 50 in (127 cm) is said to measure 12.2 hands. The table below shows recommended heights of ponies for young riders.

Pony's height (hh)	Child's age (years)
11–12	7–9
12–13	10–13
13–14.2	13–15
14.2–15.2	15–17

Odds in dice and cards
Dice

Odds in dice-throwing are determined by comparing
favorable results with unfavorable. With one die, you
have six possible results – one for each side of the die;
with two die, you have 36 possible results. Some
results – a 12 or a 2 – you have only one chance to
achieve. Thus the odds against throwing a 12 or 2 are
35 to 1. For results with two possible combinations, the
chances are 35 to 2, or 17 to 1. The table below shows
the odds for each possible combination.

Combination		Chances		Combination
2	⚀⚀	35–1	⚅⚅	12
3	⚀⚁ ⚁⚀	17–1	⚄⚅ ⚅⚄	11
4	⚂⚀ ⚀⚂ ⚁⚁	11–1	⚅⚃ ⚃⚅ ⚄⚄	10
5	⚃⚀ ⚀⚃ ⚁⚂ ⚂⚁	8.5–1	⚄⚃ ⚃⚄ ⚅⚂ ⚂⚅	9
6	⚄⚀ ⚀⚄ ⚂⚂ ⚁⚃ ⚃⚁	7–1	⚅⚁ ⚁⚅ ⚂⚃ ⚄⚂ ⚂⚄	8
7	⚅⚀ ⚀⚅ ⚄⚁ ⚁⚄ ⚂⚃ ⚃⚂	5–1		

Poker

Odds in poker are figured against a total number of possible combinations of 2,598,960. Thus, the odds of getting a royal flush (4 possible combinations) are 2,598,960 to 4, or 649,739 to 1.

Hand	Chances
royal flush	649,739 to 1
straight flush	72,192 to 1
four of a kind	4,164 to 1
full house	693 to 1
flush	508 to 1
straight	254 to 1
three of a kind	46 to 1
two pairs	20 to 1
one pair	2.4 to 1
nil	2 to 1

Blackjack (Pontoon)

There are a possible 1,326 combinations in blackjack; the odds of reaching 21 with two cards from a 52-card deck (64 possible combinations) are thus 1,326 to 64, or 21 to 1.

Two-card total	Chances
21	21 to 1
20	9 to 1
19	16.5 to 1
18	15 to 1
17	14 to 1
16	15 to 1
15	14 to 1
14	13 to 1
13	11 to 1

11: Astronomy

Planetary features

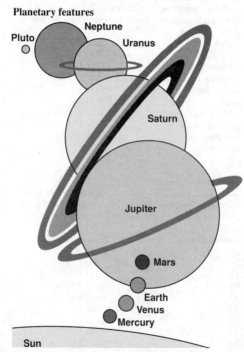

Pluto

Neptune

Uranus

Saturn

Jupiter

Mars

Earth

Venus

Mercury

Sun

Diameter at equator

Planet	mi	km
Mercury	2,926.8	4,878
Venus	7,262.4	12,104
Earth	7,653.6	12,756
Mars	4,077.0	6,795
Jupiter	85,680.0	142,800
Saturn	72,000.0	120,000
Uranus	30,480.0	50,800
Neptune	29,100.0	48,500
Pluto	1,800.0	3,000

Rotation period

Mercury	58 days 15 hr
Venus	243 days
Earth	23 hr 56 min
Mars	24 hr 37 min
Jupiter	9 hr 50 min
Saturn	10 hr 14 min
Uranus	16 hr 10 min
Neptune	18 hr 26 min
Pluto	6 days 9 hr

Average surface temperatures

Solid surface		Cloud surface	
Mercury {	662 °F (day)	Jupiter	–238 °F
	–274 °F (night)	Saturn	–292 °F
Venus	896 °F	Uranus	–346 °F
Earth	72 °F	Neptune	–364 °F
Mars	–9 °F	Pluto	–382 °F

Planetary distances

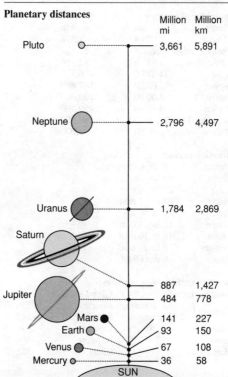

	Million mi	Million km
Pluto	3,661	5,891
Neptune	2,796	4,497
Uranus	1,784	2,869
Saturn	887	1,427
Jupiter	484	778
Mars	141	227
Earth	93	150
Venus	67	108
Mercury	36	58

SUN

Mean distance from the Sun

Planet	mi	km
Mercury	36,000,000	58,000,000
Venus	67,000,000	108,000,000
Earth	93,000,000	150,000,000
Mars	141,000,000	227,000,000
Jupiter	484,000,000	778,000,000
Saturn	887,000,000	1,427,000,000
Uranus	1,784,000,000	2,869,000,000
Neptune	2,796,000,000	4,497,000,000
Pluto	3,661,000,000	5,891,000,000

Closest distance to the Earth

Planet	mi	km
Mercury	50,000,000	80,800,000
Venus	25,000,000	40,400,000
Mars	35,000,000	56,800,000
Jupiter	367,000,000	591,000,000
Saturn	744,000,000	1,198,000,000
Uranus	1,607,000,000	2,585,000,000
Pluto*	2,670,000,000	4,297,000,000
Neptune	2,678,000,000	4,308,000,000

*Between 1979 and 1999 Pluto will be closer to the Earth than Neptune because of the unusual shape of its orbit.

The solar system – Orbits and rotation

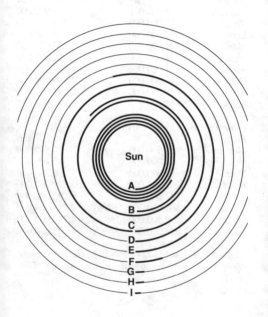

Sidereal period

Sidereal period is the time it takes a planet to orbit the Sun. Planets' orbital speeds vary, as does their distance from the Sun, so these periods are different for each planet. The diagram shows how far each planet travels in its orbit during the time it takes the Earth to complete one orbit (approximately 1 year).

		Sidereal period	Average orbital speed
A	Mercury	88.0 days	28.75 mi/s
B	Venus	224.7 days	21.7 mi/s
C	Earth	365.3 days	18.5 mi/s
D	Mars	687.0 days	14.97 mi/s
E	Jupiter	11.86 years	8.14 mi/s
F	Saturn	29.46 years	5.97 mi/s
G	Uranus	84.01 years	4.23 mi/s
H	Neptune	164.8 years	3.36 mi/s
I	Pluto	247.7 years	2.92 mi/s

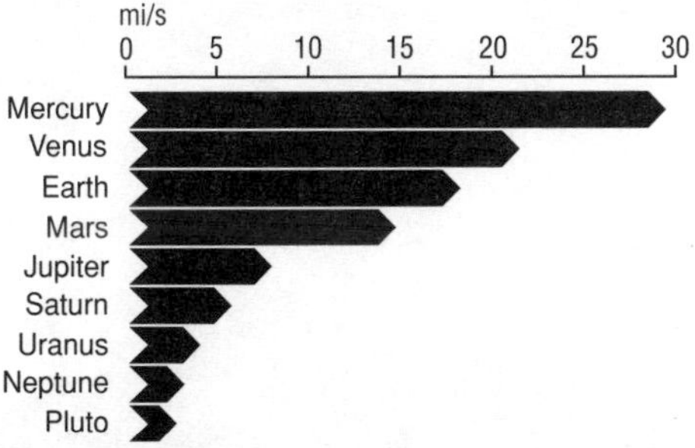

Light years

The table below lists standard abbreviations and equivalents for the units used in measuring astronomical distances. These are very large units and are related to the Earth's orbit.

A light year (ly) is the distance light travels – at its speed of 186,282 mi/s – through space over a tropical year.

An astronomical unit (au) is the mean distance between the Earth and the Sun.

A parsec (pc) is the distance at which a baseline of 1 au in length subtends an angle of 1 second.

1 au = 93,000,000 mi = 149,600,000 km
1 ly = 5,878,000,000,000 mi = 9,460,500,000,000 km
1 pc = 19,174,000,000,000 mi = 30,857,200,000,000 km
1 ly = 63,240 au
1 pc = 206,265 au = 3.262 ly

Planetary data

	Mercury	Venus	Earth
Mean distance from Sun	0.39 au	0.72 au	1.00 au
Distance at perihelion	0.31 au	0.72 au	0.98 au
Distance at aphelion	0.47 au	0.73 au	1.02 au
Closest distance to Earth	0.54 au	0.27 au	
Average orbital speed	28.75 mi/s	21.7 mi/s	18.5 mi/s
Rotation period	58 days 15 hr	243 days	23 hr 56 min
Sidereal period	88 days	224.7 days	365.3 days
Diameter at equator	3,030 mi	7,520 mi	7,926 mi
Mass (Earth's mass=1)	0.06	0.82	1
Surface temperature	662 °F (day) −274 °F (night)	896 °F	72 °F
Gravity (Earth's gravity = 1)	0.38	0.88	1
Density (density of water = 1)	5.5	5.25	5.517
Number of satellites known	0	0	1
Number of rings known	0	0	0
Main gases in atmosphere	no atmosphere	Carbon dioxide	Nitrogen, oxygen

Planetary data (continued)

	Mars	Jupiter
Mean distance from Sun	1.52 au	5.20 au
Distance at perihelion	1.38 au	4.95 au
Distance at aphelion	1.67 au	5.46 au
Closest distance to Earth	0.38 au	3.95 au
Average orbital speed	14.97 mi/s	8.14 mi/s
Rotation period	24 hr 37 min	9 hr 50 min
Sidereal period	687 days	11.86 years
Diameter at equator	4,222 mi	88,734 mi
Mass (Earth's mass=1)	0.11	317.9
Surface temperature	−9 °F	−238 °F
Gravity (Earth's gravity = 1)	0.38	2.64
Density (density of water = 1)	3.94	1.33
Number of satellites known	2	16
Number of rings known	0	1
Main gases in atmosphere	Carbon dioxide	Hydrogen, helium

Saturn	Uranus	Neptune	Pluto
9.54 au	19.18 au	30.06 au	39.36 au
9.01 au	18.28 au	29.80 au	29.58 au
10.07 au	20.09 au	30.32 au	49.14 au
8.01au	17.28 au	28.80 au	28.72 au
5.97 mi/s	4.23 mi/s	3.36 mi/s	2.92 mi/s
10 hr 14 min	16 hr 10 min	18 hr 26 min	6 days 9 hr
29.46 years	84.01 years	164.8 years	247.7 years
74,566 mi	31,566 mi	30,137 mi	3,725 mi
95.2	14.6	17.2	0.002–0.003
−292 °F	−346 °F	−364 °F	−382 °F
1.15	1.17	1.2	not known
0.71	1.7	1.77	not known
19	5	2	1
1,000+	9	0	0
Hydrogen, helium	Hydrogen, helium, methane	Hydrogen, helium, methane	Methane

12: Earth

Earth's interior
A Crust (under oceans) 4 mi (6 km) deep; made of basalt (a type of rock). Crust (continental): average 22 mi (35 km) deep; made of granite
B Mantle 1,810 mi (2,912 km) deep; probably containing peridotite (a heavy, dark rock), dunite (olivine rock), and ecologite (a dense form of basalt)
C Outer core 1,242 mi (1,999 km) deep; probably liquid iron with some dissolved sulfur and silicon
D Inner core 842 mi (1,354 km) deep; probably solid iron

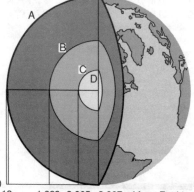

0			
13	1,823	3,065	3,907 mi from Earth's crust
21	2,933	4,932	6,286 km from Earth's crust

Atmospheric layers and depths of the Earth

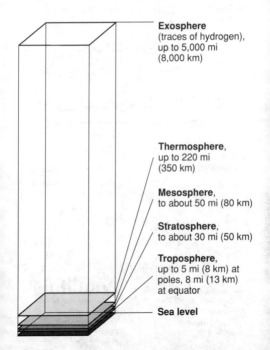

Exosphere
(traces of hydrogen),
up to 5,000 mi
(8,000 km)

Thermosphere,
up to 220 mi
(350 km)

Mesosphere,
to about 50 mi (80 km)

Stratosphere,
to about 30 mi (50 km)

Troposphere,
up to 5 mi (8 km) at
poles, 8 mi (13 km)
at equator

Sea level

Climate
The climate of a region is primarily the result of location (latitude and longitude); altitude (height above sea level); the air pressure; the wind patterns; and the rainfall.

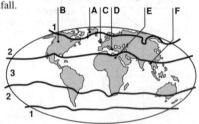

1 Polar climate zone
2 Temperate climate zone
3 Tropical climate zone

 = Rainfall (in.)

= Max. temperatures (°F)

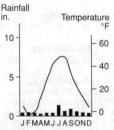

A Polar
Thule (Greenland)
Total: 4 in

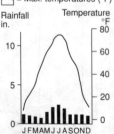

B Cold temperate (continental)
Peace River (Canada)
Total: 15 in

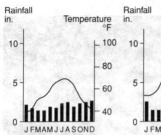

C Cool temperate (marine)
London (UK)
Total: 23 in

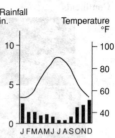

D Warm temperate
Athens (Greece)
Total: 16 in

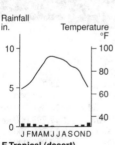

E Tropical (desert)
Cairo (Egypt)
Total: 1 in

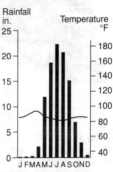

F Tropical (monsoon)
Yangon (Myanmar)
Total: 103 in

Continents

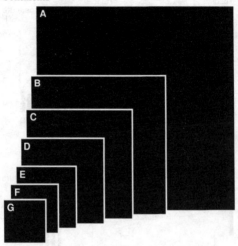

A Asia	17,085,000 mi²	44,250,000 km²
B Africa	11,685,000 mi²	30,264,000 km²
C N. America	9,420,000 mi²	24,398,000 km²
D S. America	6,870,000 mi²	17,793,000 km²
E Antarctica	5,100,000 mi²	13,209,000 km²
F Europe	3,825,000 mi²	9,907,000 km²
G Australasia	3,295,000 mi²	8,534,000 km²

Largest countries

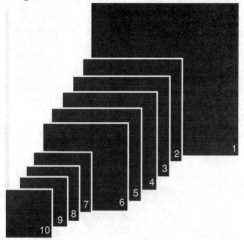

1	Russian Federation	6,593,000 mi²	17,075,000 km²
2	Canada	3,852,000 mi²	9,976,000 km²
3	China	3,692,000 mi²	9,561,000 km²
4	USA	3,676,000 mi²	9,520,000 km²
5	Brazil	3,286,000 mi²	8,512,000 km²
6	Australia	2,966,000 mi²	7,682,000 km²
7	India	1,269,000 mi²	3,288,000 km²
8	Argentina	1,072,000 mi²	2,777,000 km²
9	Sudan	968,000 mi²	2,506,000 km²
10	Zaïre	905,000 mi²	2,345,000 km²

Oceans and seas

		mi²	km²
1	Pacific Ocean	63,800,000	165,242,000
2	Atlantic Ocean	31,800,000	82,362,000
3	Indian Ocean	28,400,000	73,556,000
4	Arctic Ocean	5,400,000	13,986,000
5	South China Sea	1,149,000	2,975,000
6	Caribbean Sea	1,063,000	2,753,000
7	Mediterranean Sea	967,000	2,505,000
8	Bering Sea	876,000	2,269,000
9	Gulf of Mexico	596,000	1,544,000
10	Sea of Okhotsk	590,000	1,528,000

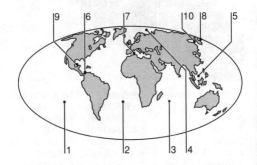

Largest (single) islands

2 New Guinea
317,000 mi²
821,000 km²

1 Greenland
840,000 mi²
2,176,000 km²

3 Borneo
287,000 mi²
743,000 km²

4 Madagascar
227,000 mi²
588,000 km²

5 Baffin (Canada)
184,000 mi²
476,000 km²

7= Honshu (Japan)
89,000 mi²
230,000 km²

7= Great Britain
89,000 mi²
230,000 km²

9 Victoria (Canada)
82,200 mi²   213,000 km²

10 Ellesmere (Canada)
81,800 mi²
212,000 km²

6 Sumatra
183,000 mi²
474,000 km²

Volcanoes and mountains

Highest volcanoes

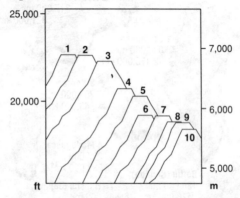

1	Ojos del Salado	S. America	22,590 ft	6,885 m
2	Pissis	S. America	22,580 ft	6,882 m
3	Llullaillaco*	S. America	22,110 ft	6,739 m
4	Chimborazo	S. America	20,703 ft	6,310 m
5	McKinley	N. America	20,320 ft	6,194 m
6	Cotopaxi†	S. America	19,344 ft	5,896 m
7	Kilimanjaro	Africa	19,340 ft	5,895 m
8	Antisana†	S. America	18,892 ft	5,758 m
9	Citlaltepetl	N. America	18,853 ft	5,746 m
10	Elbrus	Europe	18,480 ft	5,633 m
*Quiescent		†Active		

Highest mountains

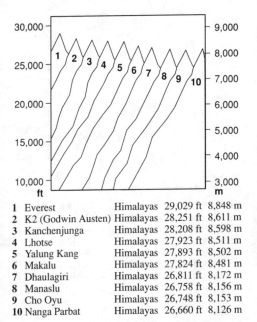

#		Range	Height (ft)	Height (m)
1	Everest	Himalayas	29,029 ft	8,848 m
2	K2 (Godwin Austen)	Himalayas	28,251 ft	8,611 m
3	Kanchenjunga	Himalayas	28,208 ft	8,598 m
4	Lhotse	Himalayas	27,923 ft	8,511 m
5	Yalung Kang	Himalayas	27,893 ft	8,502 m
6	Makalu	Himalayas	27,824 ft	8,481 m
7	Dhaulagiri	Himalayas	26,811 ft	8,172 m
8	Manaslu	Himalayas	26,758 ft	8,156 m
9	Cho Oyu	Himalayas	26,748 ft	8,153 m
10	Nanga Parbat	Himalayas	26,660 ft	8,126 m

Highest mountain in each continent

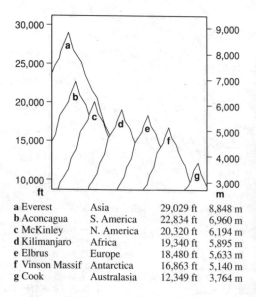

a	Everest	Asia	29,029 ft	8,848 m
b	Aconcagua	S. America	22,834 ft	6,960 m
c	McKinley	N. America	20,320 ft	6,194 m
d	Kilimanjaro	Africa	19,340 ft	5,895 m
e	Elbrus	Europe	18,480 ft	5,633 m
f	Vinson Massif	Antarctica	16,863 ft	5,140 m
g	Cook	Australasia	12,349 ft	3,764 m

Highest mountain in selected countries

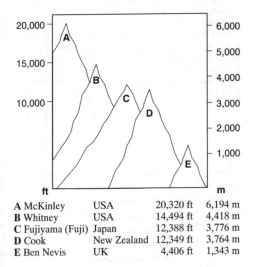

A	McKinley	USA	20,320 ft	6,194 m
B	Whitney	USA	14,494 ft	4,418 m
C	Fujiyama (Fuji)	Japan	12,388 ft	3,776 m
D	Cook	New Zealand	12,349 ft	3,764 m
E	Ben Nevis	UK	4,406 ft	1,343 m

Longest rivers

1	Nile	Africa	4,132 mi	6,650 km
2	Amazon	S. America	4,000 mi	6,437 km
3	Mississippi-Missouri-Red Rock	N. America	3,860 mi	6,212 km
4	Ob-Irtysh	Asia	3,461 mi	5,570 km
5	Yangtze (Chang)	Asia	3,430 mi	5,520 km
6	Huang He	Asia	2,903 mi	4,672 km
7	Congo (Zaire)	Africa	2,900 mi	4,667 km
8	Amur	Asia	2,802 mi	4,509 km
9	Lena	Asia	2,653 mi	4,270 km
10	Mackenzie	N. America	2,635 mi	4,241 km

Longest in its continent

A Africa	Nile		4,132 mi	6,650 km
B S. America	Amazon		4,000 mi	6,437 km
C N. America	Mississippi- Missouri- Red Rock		3,860 mi	6,212 km
D Asia	Ob-Irtysh		3,461 mi	5,570 km
E Europe	Volga		2,293 mi	3,690 km
F Australasia	Murray		2,000 mi	3,219 km

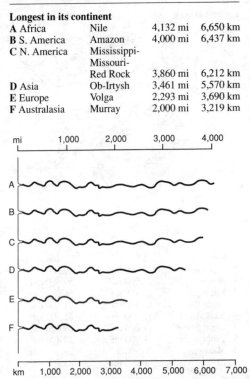

Largest lakes

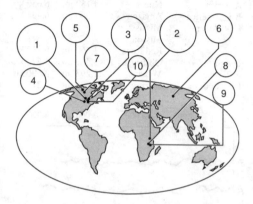

1	Superior	31,800 mi²	82,400 km²
2	Victoria	26,800 mi²	69,500 km²
3	Huron	23,000 mi²	59,600 km²
4	Michigan	22,400 mi²	58,000 km²
5	Great Bear	12,300 mi²	31,800 km²
6	Baykal	12,200 mi²	31,500 km²
7	Great Slave	11,000 mi²	28,400 km²
8	Tanganyika	11,000 mi²	28,400 km²
9	Malawi	10,900 mi²	28,200 km²
10	Erie	9,900 mi²	25,700 km²

Largest waterfalls

1 Angel, Venezuela
3,212 ft (979 m)

2 Tugela, S. Africa
3,110 ft (948 m)

3 Utigőrd, Norway
2,625 ft (800 m)

4 Mongefossen, Norway
2,540 ft (774 m)

5 Yosemite, USA
2,425 ft (739 m)

6 Østre Mardøla Foss,
Norway
2,154 ft (657 m)

7 Tyssestrengane, Norway
2,120 ft (646 m)

8 Kukenaom, Venezuela
2,000 ft (610 m)

9 Sutherland, N. Zealand
1,904 ft (580 m)

10 Kjellfossen, Norway
1,841 ft (561 m)

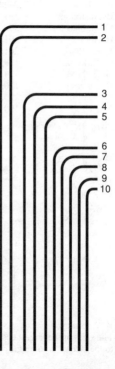

Largest deserts

A	Sahara	3,242,000 mi²	8,397,000 km²
B	Australian	598,000 mi²	1,549,000 km²
C	Arabian	502,000 mi²	1,300,000 km²
D	Gobi	401,000 mi²	1,039,000 km²
E	Kalahari	201,000 mi²	521,000 km²
F	Turkestan	139,000 mi²	360,000 km²
G	Takla Makan	124,000 mi²	321,000 km²
H	Sonoran	120,000 mi²	311,000 km²
I	Namib	120,000 mi²	311,000 km²
J	Thar	100,000 mi²	259,000 km²

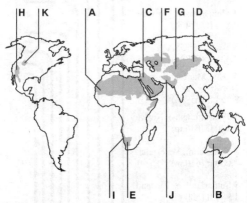

K Wyoming   98,000 mi²   254,000 km²
The sizes of the largest deserts are compared (opposite)
to the size of Wyoming.

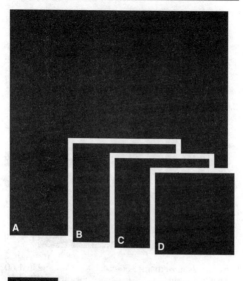

Deepest caves

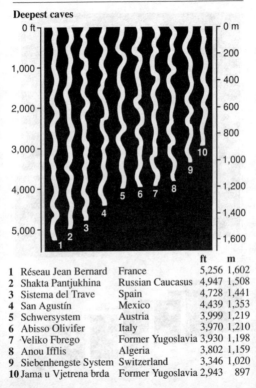

			ft	m
1	Réseau Jean Bernard	France	5,256	1,602
2	Shakta Pantjukhina	Russian Caucasus	4,947	1,508
3	Sistema del Trave	Spain	4,728	1,441
4	San Agustín	Mexico	4,439	1,353
5	Schwersystem	Austria	3,999	1,219
6	Abisso Olivifer	Italy	3,970	1,210
7	Veliko Fbrego	Former Yugoslavia	3,930	1,198
8	Anou Ifflis	Algeria	3,802	1,159
9	Siebenhengste System	Switzerland	3,346	1,020
10	Jama u Vjetrena brda	Former Yugoslavia	2,943	897

Capitals of the world
Africa
ALGERIA Algiers
ANGOLA Luanda
BENIN Porto-Novo
BOTSWANA Gaborone
BURKINA FASO
  Ouagadougou
BURUNDI Bujumbura
CAMEROON Yaoundé
CAPE VERDE Praia
CENTRAL AFRICAN
REPUBLIC Bangui
CHAD N'Djamena
COMOROS Moroni
CONGO Brazzaville
DJIBOUTI Djibouti
EGYPT Cairo
EQUATORIAL GUINEA
  Malabo
ERITREA Asmara
ETHIOPIA Addis Ababa
GABON Libreville
GAMBIA Banjul
GHANA Accra
GUINEA Conakry
GUINEA-BISSAU
  Bissau
IVORY COAST
(CÔTE D'IVOIRE)
  Yamoussoukro/Abidjan
KENYA Nairobi

LESOTHO Maseru
LIBERIA Monrovia
LIBYA Tripoli
MADAGASCAR
  Antananarivo
MALAWI Lilongwe
MALI Bamako
MAURITANIA
  Nouakchott
MAURITIUS Port Louis
MOROCCO Rabat
MOZAMBIQUE Maputo
NAMIBIA Windhoek
NIGER Niamey
NIGERIA Abuja
RWANDA Kigali
SÃO TOMÉ AND
PRÍNCIPE São Tomé
SENEGAL Dakar
SEYCHELLES Victoria
SIERRA LEONE Freetown
SOMALIA Mogadishu
SOUTH AFRICA
  Cape Town/ Pretoria
SUDAN Khartoum
SWAZILAND Mbabane
TANZANIA Dodoma
TOGO Lomé
TUNISIA Tunis
UGANDA Kampala
ZAÏRE Kinshasa
ZAMBIA Lusaka

ZIMBABWE Harare

Asia and Middle East
AFGHANISTAN Kabul
BAHRAIN Manama
BANGLADESH Dhaka
BHUTAN Thimphu
BRUNEI Bandar Seri
  Begawan
CAMBODIA
  Phnom Penh
CHINA Beijing
INDIA New Delhi
INDONESIA Jakarta
IRAN Tehran
IRAQ Baghdad
ISRAEL Jerusalem
JAPAN Tokyo
JORDAN Amman
KAZAKHSTAN Alma-
  Ata
KIRGHIZIA Frunze
KOREA, NORTH
  Pyongyang
KOREA, SOUTH Seoul
KUWAIT Kuwait City
LAOS Vientiane
LEBANON Beirut
MALAYSIA
  Kuala Lumpur
MALDIVES Malé
MONGOLIA Ulan Bator

MYANMAR(Burma)
  Yangon (Rangoon)
NEPAL Kathmandu
OMAN Muscat
PAKISTAN Islamabad
PHILIPPINES Manila
QATAR Doha
SAUDI ARABIA Riyadh
SINGAPORE Singapore
SRI LANKA Colombo
SYRIA Damascus
TADZHIKISTAN
  Dushanbe
THAILAND Bangkok
TURKMENISTAN
  Ashkhabad
UNITED ARAB
  EMIRATES Abu Dhabi
UZBEKISTAN Tashkent
VIETNAM Hanoi
YEMEN Sana'a

Europe
ALBANIA Tirana
ANDORRA
  Andorra la Vella
ARMENIA Yerevan
AUSTRIA Vienna
AZERBAIJAN Baku
BELARUS Minsk
BELGIUM Brussels

BOSNIA-HERZEGOVINA Sarajevo
BULGARIA Sofia
CROATIA Zagreb
CYPRUS Nicosia
CZECH REPUBLIC Prague
DENMARK Copenhagen
ESTONIA Tallinn
FINLAND Helsinki
FRANCE Paris
GEORGIA Tbilisi
GERMANY Berlin
GREECE Athens
HUNGARY Budapest
ICELAND Reykjavík
IRELAND (Eire) Dublin
ITALY Rome
LATVIA Riga
LIECHTENSTEIN Vaduz
LITHUANIA Vilnius
LUXEMBOURG Luxembourg
MACEDONIA Skopje
MALTA Valletta
MOLDOVA Kishinev
MONACO Monaco-Ville
NETHERLANDS The Hague/Amsterdam
NORWAY Oslo
POLAND Warsaw
PORTUGAL Lisbon
ROMANIA Bucharest
RUSSIA Moscow
SAN MARINO San Marino
SLOVAKIA Bratislava
SLOVENIA Ljubljana
SPAIN Madrid
SWEDEN Stockholm
SWITZERLAND Bern
TURKEY Ankara
UKRAINE Kiev
UNITED KINGDOM London
VATICAN CITY Vatican city
YUGOSLAVIA Belgrade

Australasia
AUSTRALIA Canberra
FIJI Suva
KIRIBATI Tarawa
MARSHALL ISLANDS Dalap-Uliga-Darrit
MICRONESIA Kolonia
NAURU Yaren
NEW ZEALAND Wellington
PALAU Koror
PAPUA NEW GUINEA Port Moresby

SOLOMON ISLANDS
   Honiara
TONGA Nuku'alofa
TUVALU Funafuti
VANUATU Port-Vila
WESTERN SAMOA Apia

South America
ARGENTINA Buenos
   Aires
BOLIVIA La Paz/Sucre
BRAZIL Brasília
CHILE Santiago
COLOMBIA Bogotá
ECUADOR Quito
FRENCH GUIANA
   Cayenne
GUYANA Georgetown
PARAGUAY Asunción
PERU Lima
SURINAME Paramaribo
URUGUAY Montevideo
VENEZUELA Caracas

**North and Central
America**
ANTIGUA AND
   BARBUDA St. John's
BAHAMAS Nassau
BARBADOS Bridgetown
BELIZE Belmopan

CANADA Ottawa
COSTA RICA San José
CUBA Havana
DOMINICA Roseau
DOMINICAN
REPUBLIC Santo
   Domingo
EL SALVADOR
   San Salvador
GREENLAND Nuuk
GRENADA St. George's
GUATEMALA
   Guatemala City
HAITI Port-au-Prince
HONDURAS
   Tegucigalpa
JAMAICA Kingston
MEXICO Mexico City
NICARAGUA Managua
PANAMA Panama City
ST. LUCIA Castries
ST. CHRISTOPHER
   AND NEVIS Basseterre
ST. VINCENT AND THE
   GRENADINES
   Kingstown
TRINIDAD AND
   TOBAGO Port of Spain
UNITED STATES OF
   AMERICA
   Washington D.C.